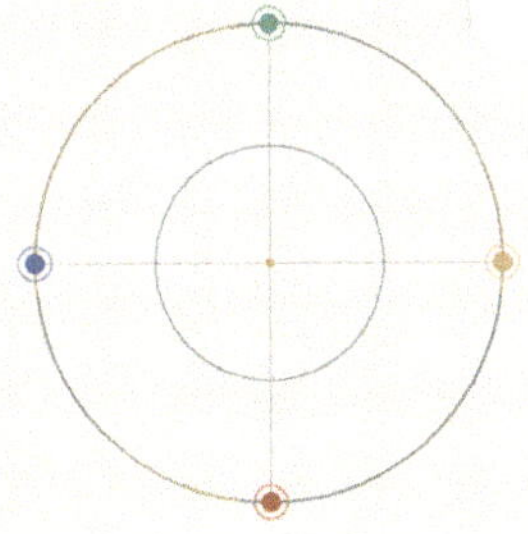

A WORKBOOK FOR

THE
TIMING
WOUND

*Sacred Return and the End of
Perpetual Offering*

KRISTI HALL

The Timing Wound: A Workbook
Sacred Return and the End of Perpetual Offering

Published by Grist
gristtheology.com

A note on craft and AI: This workbook was authored by Kristi Hall. Portions of the production process — typesetting, layout, copy editing, and structural drafting — were aided by AI tools under the author's direction. All theological content, framework, voice, and final editorial decisions are the author's.

This workbook is a companion to *The Timing Wound: Sacred Return and the End of Perpetual Offering* (Grist). The framework it operates on is developed in the book; the workbook is where the framework meets your year.

First Edition. Printed in the United States of America.

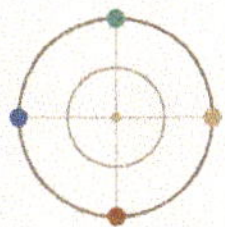

For those whose offering

has gone on longer

than its season.

TABLE OF CONTENTS

WHAT THIS WORKBOOK IS FOR

This workbook is not a self-help instrument. It is a diagnostic and repair structure for a specific theological problem: the wound that forms when a life is asked to offer continuously, without the sacred withdrawal that an arc requires to complete.

The book it accompanies — *The Timing Wound* — names that problem. It traces the God's arc through the four phases of continuity: Becoming, Authority, Offering, Return. It argues that modern life has collapsed Return — the season of withdrawal, fallow, consolidation — into a brief decompression between offerings, and that the cost of this collapse is what we call burnout. The book makes the argument. This workbook is where the argument meets your year.

The workbook depends on the book. The framework is named here in summary, but the theological development that makes the framework *work* is in *The Timing Wound* itself. Read the book first, or read it alongside this — but read it.

WHAT YOU WILL DO

You will work through four parts in order. Part One gives you the diagnostic instruments — a Season Finder you will use repeatedly, and a Wheel Plan you will draft once and revise across the year. Part Two is the deeper diagnostic — four exercises for naming the specific shape of your timing wound. Part Three is where you build the four repair tools: a rhythm rule, a gate, a constraint clause, and a closing rite. Part Four is a year-long companion journal for using those tools in the actual weather of your life.

The whole work, taken at the pace it asks, is roughly one calendar year. You will not finish it in a weekend, and you should not try. The pace is part of the point.

A FEW THINGS TO KNOW

The journal is undated. You begin where you are. Whether you start at Imbolc or Beltane or the middle of a Tuesday, the year-long companion in Part Four meets you there.

Some pages are landscape. Where a worksheet needs the full breadth of the page — most tables, the Rhythm Rule template, the Gate Builder — the page rotates. A small mark in the upper-left tells you when to turn the book.

The writing space is meant to be used. The lines are not decoration. The Notes sections are not optional. The pages that look spare are spare on purpose. The pages that look dense are asking you to be specific.

You will likely not finish every page. That is expected. A page skipped is a page you can come back to. A page half-filled is a record of where you were when you tried. The workbook does not require completion to do its work. It requires return.

ONE LAST THING

The timing wound is not a personal failing. It is a structural condition of how most of us have been asked to live. Naming it will not, by itself, repair it. What naming does is make repair possible — by giving you the words for what you are actually experiencing, and the tools for working with it.

Begin where you are. The Wheel will keep turning whether or not you are reading these pages. Your task is not to make it turn. Your task is to recognize where in its turning you actually are, and to live there honestly.

You are not late. You are where you are.

— Kristi Hall

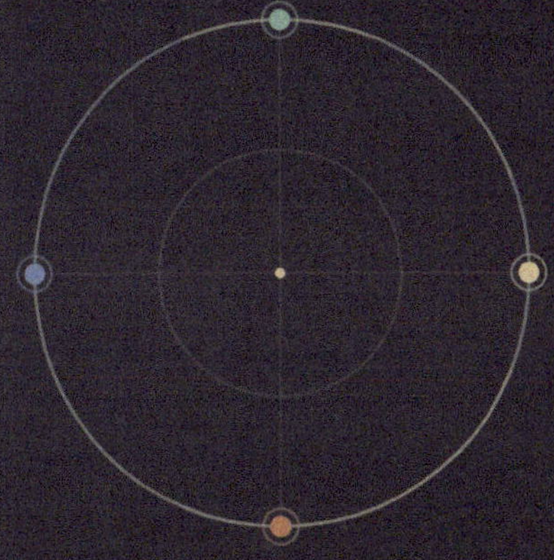

PART ONE

DIAGNOSTIC FOUNDATION

Before repair, recognition. The instruments in this section help you locate the season you are actually in — across the whole of a life, and inside each domain that asks something of you.

THE FOUR SEASONS

The God's arc names four phases of continuity. Each has a discipline and a distortion. Use this page to recognize where you are — not where you wish to be.

● BECOMING

Forming. Hidden. Not yet ripe.

- Drawn toward something not yet articulable
- Absorbing more than producing
- Tender, easily overwhelmed by exposure
- Visibility feels destabilizing, not exciting
- *Discipline:* protection. *Distortion:* being demanded to perform too soon.

● AUTHORITY

Steady. Governing. Holding continuity.

- What was begun is now sustained
- You are responsible for keeping things in order
- Power lies in reliability, not novelty
- Boundaries are gates, not walls
- *Discipline:* governance. *Distortion:* overfunctioning, control.

● OFFERING

Ripe. Released. Given with a gate.

- Something has matured and is being delivered outward
- Generative, but the gate matters more than the gift
- Ends as deliberately as it begins
- Continuity gives from surplus, not from depletion
- *Discipline:* consecrated release. *Distortion:* perpetual giving.

● RETURN

Withdrawn. Fallow. Restoring viability.

- You are depleted, quieter, asking less of yourself
- The work is not productive, and that is the work
- Withdrawal is chosen before collapse demands it
- What looks empty is preparing the next arc
- *Discipline:* consolidation. *Distortion:* avoidance, indefinite drift.

THE WHEEL OF THE YEAR

The God's arc through the four phases of continuity

Each phase has a discipline. Each sabbat marks a passage.
The Wheel turns whether or not we recognize it.

USING THE SEASON FINDER

The Season Finder is the spine of this workbook. Use it once a season — at each of the four turning points of your year — and whenever your sense of timing feels misaligned. It will not give you answers. It will give you a more honest picture of the question.

HOW THE DIAGNOSTIC WORKS

Each Season Finder is a three-step diagnostic, with each step on its own page so you can sit with it. Step One names your global season. Step Two maps how that season is showing up across each domain of your life. Step Three asks what the pattern is telling you, and where the most urgent repair lives.

After each step, you'll find a Notes section. Use it. The diagnostic is not a checklist — it is a conversation with the truth of your year, and the truth often shows up in what you write *after* the questions, not what you mark inside them.

A Note on Honesty

The most common error in this diagnostic is to mark the season you wish you were in. The second most common is to mark the season others would expect of you. Neither will help. The Season Finder works only when you let it tell you what is actually true — including the truths you would rather not see.

The season that makes you slightly uncomfortable is often the true one.

GLOBAL SEASON

Here is Step One filled in by someone else — a teacher in her late thirties, eight months into a sustained Offering season at work, with a body that is asking for something different.

MY GLOBAL SEASON RIGHT NOW

☐ **Becoming** — something is forming but not yet ready. I am absorbing more than producing.

☐ **Authority** — things are steady but demanding. I am holding a lot in place.

■ **Offering** — something is ripe. I am giving, delivering, creating outwardly. *The work is real, but it needs a gate.*

☐ **Return** — I am depleted, withdrawn, asking for rest.

HER NOTES

"I almost marked Authority. That is the answer I keep wanting — it sounds like what a teacher in her fifteenth year should be. Steady. Holding things in place. I wrote it in pencil, looked at it, and knew. Authority is the season I am performing. Offering is the season I am in. I have been in delivery mode for eight months and have not closed one gate."

II MAP YOUR DOMAINS

Here is the same teacher's domain map. Notice how the domains are not all in the same season — and how naming each one's actual season changes what becomes possible.

DOMAIN	SEASON	CURRENT DEMAND (ONE SENTENCE)	RIGHT POSTURE	ONE REPAIR THIS WEEK
Work	● Offering	Heavy delivery cycle through end of term.	Offer with a gate	End each day at 5:30 — phone off.
Body	● Return	Sleep is shallow. Energy is borrowed.	Withdraw	One unscheduled afternoon this week.
Partnership	● Authority	Steady but I am not present in it.	Govern	Saturday morning protected for us.
Creative work	● Becoming	Something is forming. I keep abandoning it.	Protect	No new commitments. Hold the question.
Community	● Offering	Two committees. Both real, neither urgent.	Offer with a gate	Step down from one by month's end.

HER NOTES

"I almost wrote 'Authority' for Partnership because we are not fighting and the logistics are working. But 'steady' is not the same as alive. I am holding the shape of it without bringing myself to it."

III READ THE PATTERN

With Step One and Step Two named, the pattern tells the truth Step Three is asking for. Here is what she saw.

HOW MANY DOMAINS ARE IN EXPANSION?

Three — work, partnership, and community. Partnership is the quietest of the three but it still costs energy to hold steady.

IF MORE THAN TWO, WHICH CAN SHIFT INTO PRESERVATION THIS WEEK?

Community. Stepping down from one committee will not break anything, and it gives body and creative work the room they need.

IS RETURN PRESENT IN ANY DOMAIN? IF NOT, WHERE CAN IT BEGIN?

Only in body, and only because the body is forcing it. The most urgent repair is honoring it before it becomes collapse.

HER SYNTHESIS

"The pattern is clearer than I expected. I have been offering from a body in Return. That is the timing wound, named. The repair is not 'rest more.' The repair is to stop offering from the seed."

NOTES

FIRST QUARTER · STEP ONE
GLOBAL SEASON

Read the four short descriptions below. Mark the one that matches your overall condition right now — not the one you want to be true, not the one others would expect. The one that is.

MY GLOBAL SEASON RIGHT NOW

☐ **Becoming** — something is forming but not yet ready. I am absorbing more than producing. I need protection, not exposure.

☐ **Authority** — things are steady but demanding. I am holding a lot in place. I need governance, limits, containment — not new projects.

☐ **Offering** — something is ripe. I am giving, delivering, creating outwardly. The work is real, but it needs a gate.

☐ **Return** — I am depleted, withdrawn, asking for rest. My system is signaling that demand must decrease. I need fallow, not more effort.

NOTES

____

____

____

____

____

____

____

II MAP YOUR DOMAINS

List four to six domains that are asking something of you right now: work, parenting, partnership, body, home, creative work, community. Beside each, mark its season, name the demand in one sentence, name the right posture, and one specific repair you can make this week.

DOMAIN	SEASON	CURRENT DEMAND (ONE SENTENCE)	RIGHT POSTURE	ONE REPAIR THIS WEEK

NOTES

ROTATE TO READ

III READ THE PATTERN

The pattern across your domains tells a story. Read it. Where is expansion concentrated? Where is Return missing? Which one shift this week would change the most?

HOW MANY DOMAINS ARE IN EXPANSION?

____

IF MORE THAN TWO, WHICH ONE CAN SHIFT INTO PRESERVATION THIS WEEK?

____

____

IS RETURN PRESENT IN ANY DOMAIN? IF NOT, WHERE CAN IT BEGIN?

____

____

WHAT IS THE ONE REPAIR THIS WEEK THAT WOULD CHANGE THE MOST?

____

____

NOTES ____

____

____

NOTES

SECOND QUARTER · STEP ONE
GLOBAL SEASON

Read the four short descriptions below. Mark the one that matches your overall condition right now — not the one you want to be true, not the one others would expect. The one that is.

MY GLOBAL SEASON RIGHT NOW

☐ **Becoming** — something is forming but not yet ready. I am absorbing more than producing. I need protection, not exposure.

☐ **Authority** — things are steady but demanding. I am holding a lot in place. I need governance, limits, containment — not new projects.

☐ **Offering** — something is ripe. I am giving, delivering, creating outwardly. The work is real, but it needs a gate.

☐ **Return** — I am depleted, withdrawn, asking for rest. My system is signaling that demand must decrease. I need fallow, not more effort.

NOTES

____

____

____

____

____

____

II MAP YOUR DOMAINS

List four to six domains that are asking something of you right now: work, parenting, partnership, body, home, creative work, community. Beside each, mark its season, name the demand in one sentence, name the right posture, and one specific repair you can make this week.

DOMAIN	SEASON	CURRENT DEMAND (ONE SENTENCE)	RIGHT POSTURE	ONE REPAIR THIS WEEK

NOTES

ROTATE TO READ

III SECOND QUARTER · STEP THREE
READ THE PATTERN

The pattern across your domains tells a story. Read it. Where is expansion concentrated? Where is Return missing? Which one shift this week would change the most?

HOW MANY DOMAINS ARE IN EXPANSION?

____

IF MORE THAN TWO, WHICH ONE CAN SHIFT INTO
PRESERVATION THIS WEEK?

____

____

IS RETURN PRESENT IN ANY DOMAIN? IF NOT, WHERE
CAN IT BEGIN?

____

____

WHAT IS THE ONE REPAIR THIS WEEK THAT WOULD
CHANGE THE MOST?

____

____

NOTES ____________________________________

____

____

NOTES

THIRD QUARTER · STEP ONE
GLOBAL SEASON

Read the four short descriptions below. Mark the one that matches your overall condition right now — not the one you want to be true, not the one others would expect. The one that is.

MY GLOBAL SEASON RIGHT NOW

☐ **Becoming** — something is forming but not yet ready. I am absorbing more than producing. I need protection, not exposure.

☐ **Authority** — things are steady but demanding. I am holding a lot in place. I need governance, limits, containment — not new projects.

☐ **Offering** — something is ripe. I am giving, delivering, creating outwardly. The work is real, but it needs a gate.

☐ **Return** — I am depleted, withdrawn, asking for rest. My system is signaling that demand must decrease. I need fallow, not more effort.

NOTES

II MAP YOUR DOMAINS

List four to six domains that are asking something of you right now: work, parenting, partnership, body, home, creative work, community. Beside each, mark its season, name the demand in one sentence, name the right posture, and one specific repair you can make this week.

DOMAIN	SEASON	CURRENT DEMAND (ONE SENTENCE)	RIGHT POSTURE	ONE REPAIR THIS WEEK

NOTES

ROTATE TO READ

III THIRD QUARTER · STEP THREE
READ THE PATTERN

The pattern across your domains tells a story. Read it. Where is expansion concentrated? Where is Return missing? Which one shift this week would change the most?

HOW MANY DOMAINS ARE IN EXPANSION?

____

IF MORE THAN TWO, WHICH ONE CAN SHIFT INTO
PRESERVATION THIS WEEK?

____

____

IS RETURN PRESENT IN ANY DOMAIN? IF NOT, WHERE
CAN IT BEGIN?

____

____

WHAT IS THE ONE REPAIR THIS WEEK THAT WOULD
CHANGE THE MOST?

____

____

____

NOTES ____

____

____

NOTES

FOURTH QUARTER · STEP ONE
GLOBAL SEASON

Read the four short descriptions below. Mark the one that matches your overall condition right now — not the one you want to be true, not the one others would expect. The one that is.

MY GLOBAL SEASON RIGHT NOW

☐ **Becoming** — something is forming but not yet ready. I am absorbing more than producing. I need protection, not exposure.

☐ **Authority** — things are steady but demanding. I am holding a lot in place. I need governance, limits, containment — not new projects.

☐ **Offering** — something is ripe. I am giving, delivering, creating outwardly. The work is real, but it needs a gate.

☐ **Return** — I am depleted, withdrawn, asking for rest. My system is signaling that demand must decrease. I need fallow, not more effort.

NOTES

II MAP YOUR DOMAINS

List four to six domains that are asking something of you right now: work, parenting, partnership, body, home, creative work, community. Beside each, mark its season, name the demand in one sentence, name the right posture, and one specific repair you can make this week.

DOMAIN	SEASON	CURRENT DEMAND (ONE SENTENCE)	RIGHT POSTURE	ONE REPAIR THIS WEEK

NOTES

ROTATE TO READ

III FOURTH QUARTER · STEP THREE
READ THE PATTERN

The pattern across your domains tells a story. Read it. Where is expansion concentrated? Where is Return missing? Which one shift this week would change the most?

HOW MANY DOMAINS ARE IN EXPANSION?

____

IF MORE THAN TWO, WHICH ONE CAN SHIFT INTO PRESERVATION THIS WEEK?

____

____

IS RETURN PRESENT IN ANY DOMAIN? IF NOT, WHERE CAN IT BEGIN?

____

____

WHAT IS THE ONE REPAIR THIS WEEK THAT WOULD CHANGE THE MOST?

____

____

NOTES ____________________________________

____

NOTES

THE PERSONAL WHEEL PLAN

Where the Season Finder is a snapshot, the Wheel Plan is a map. It names the shape of your year as your actual constraints and commitments are making it.

WHAT THE PLAN ASKS OF YOU

The next three pages walk you through the plan in order. The Wheel Plan is not a productivity calendar. It is a structural diagnosis of where Offering will likely occur this year, which domains will need to hold Authority while that Offering happens, and where Return must be scheduled so the year can close honestly.

Page one — Domains and seasons

Map your four to six primary domains. Beside each, name the shape that domain will take this year: a season of Becoming, a season of Authority, a season of Offering, a season of Return.

Page two — Offerings and returns

Name the specific offerings — projects, deliveries, presences — that this year will require. Beside each, name the Return that makes it survivable.

Page three — Constraint clause

Predeclare what you will do when pressure increases. The clause prevents the most common burnout reaction: pressure rises, so you add more.

What you map here is the year as it is asking to be lived — its offerings and returns already forming.

1 DOMAINS AND SEASONS

Name four to six domains. For each, mark the dominant season this year. A domain may pass through several — but commit to the dominant one. That is the season that will govern your structural decisions.

DOMAIN	BEC.	AUTH.	OFF.	RET.	NOTES — WHAT THIS DOMAIN WILL ASK OF ME

ROTATE TO READ

DOMAINS AND SEASONS · REFLECTION

Read back the map you just drew. What does the year actually look like when you see it whole?

WHICH DOMAIN IS THE PRIMARY OFFERING THIS YEAR?

Only one domain can hold the year's primary offering. The others support it, hold steady, or rest. Name the one.

____

____

____

____

WHERE IS BECOMING LIVING — WHAT NEEDS PROTECTION?

What is forming this year that has not yet earned its own authority — and must therefore be kept from the demand to perform before it is ready?

____

____

____

____

OFFERINGS AND RETURNS

Name each major offering this year will require. Beside it, name the structural Return that makes it survivable — the deliberate withdrawal that lets the next offering begin clean.

● OFFERING — WHAT IS BEING DELIVERED   WHEN   ● RETURN — WHAT CLOSES IT

SCHEDULED FALLOW

Place Return into the year as structural commitment. Fallow weeks, decompression windows, weekly withdrawals — written into the calendar before anything else fills it.

FALLOW MONTH OR EXTENDED RETURN

A multi-week span this year that holds no offering. When does it fall, and what makes it possible?

QUARTERLY DECOMPRESSION WINDOWS

The week after each quarter ends. What closes the quarter, and what does the decompression look like in practice?

WEEKLY RETURN — WHAT DAY, WHAT SHAPE

The day each week that holds no production. Name it, and name what it actually contains.

THE CONSTRAINT CLAUSE

Real life will interrupt this plan. Constraint will increase. Predeclaring how you respond is the difference between a hard season and a collapse.

NAME WHAT WILL CONSTRAIN YOU

Financial pressure, caregiving load, illness, deadline, difficult relationship. Constraint is structural, not failure.

____

____

____

MY CONSTRAINT CLAUSE

Write the rule you commit to in advance. The clause works because it is decided before the pressure arrives.

____

____

____

____

PERSONAL WHEEL PLAN · CONSTRAINT CLAUSE (CONTINUED)

FIRST TO CUT, LAST TO CUT

What is the first commitment you will release when pressure rises? What protects everything else and must be defended last?

I FIRST QUARTERLY RE-CHECK
WHAT HAS SHIFTED?

The Wheel Plan was a map of the year as you saw it then. A quarter has passed. Some of it was right. Some of it was wrong. What is the year actually asking of you now?

WHAT WAS RIGHT ABOUT THE PLAN

____

____

____

WHAT WAS WRONG

____

____

____

WHAT HAS SHIFTED SEASON?

A domain in Authority is now Offering. A domain in Becoming has begun governing. Name the shift.

____

____

____

II SECOND QUARTERLY RE-CHECK
WHAT HAS SHIFTED?

The Wheel Plan was a map of the year as you saw it then. A quarter has passed. Some of it was right. Some of it was wrong. What is the year actually asking of you now?

WHAT WAS RIGHT ABOUT THE PLAN

____

____

____

WHAT WAS WRONG

____

____

____

WHAT HAS SHIFTED SEASON?

A domain in Authority is now Offering. A domain in Becoming has begun governing. Name the shift.

____

____

____

III   THIRD QUARTERLY RE-CHECK
WHAT HAS SHIFTED?

The Wheel Plan was a map of the year as you saw it then. A quarter has passed. Some of it was right. Some of it was wrong. What is the year actually asking of you now?

WHAT WAS RIGHT ABOUT THE PLAN

____

____

____

____

WHAT WAS WRONG

____

____

____

WHAT HAS SHIFTED SEASON?

A domain in Authority is now Offering. A domain in Becoming has begun governing. Name the shift.

____

____

____

IV — FOURTH QUARTERLY RE-CHECK
WHAT HAS SHIFTED?

The Wheel Plan was a map of the year as you saw it then. A quarter has passed. Some of it was right. Some of it was wrong. What is the year actually asking of you now?

WHAT WAS RIGHT ABOUT THE PLAN

WHAT WAS WRONG

WHAT HAS SHIFTED SEASON?

A domain in Authority is now Offering. A domain in Becoming has begun governing. Name the shift.

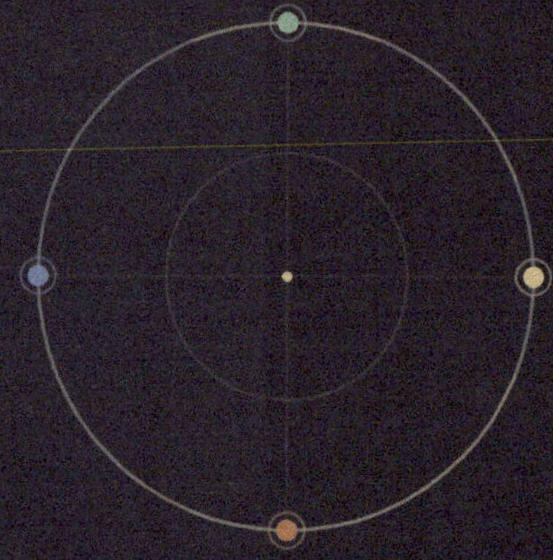

SELF- ASSESSMENT

Four exercises for naming the specific shape of your timing wound. Where you are offering before something is ripe. Where sacred time has collapsed. Which violation you are committing. Which season you are acting from.

I PART TWO · CHAPTER ONE

PREMATURE SACRIFICE

The most common timing wound is offering from a seed that has not yet ripened. The work goes out before it is ready. The relationship asks for delivery before its foundation has set. The body is taxed before its strength has been built.

Premature sacrifice is not failure of will. It is failure of timing. It happens when external pressure or internal anxiety overrides the slow ripening that an offering requires. The result is not just depletion — it is the collapse of the offering itself, which arrives half-formed because it was made to arrive.

THE FOUR SIGNS

You may be in premature sacrifice if any of these are true:

- You are delivering work that does not feel like yours yet, or that you cannot yet stand behind without explanation.

- You are explaining your offering as you make it — apologizing in advance for what it is not yet.

- The deadline came from outside, and the work shaped itself around the deadline rather than its own ripening.

- You feel a private knowing that what you are giving is not yet what it could be — and you are giving it anyway.

The fruit picked too early ripens off the tree, but it does not ripen well.

WHAT ARE YOU OFFERING RIGHT NOW?

List the offerings you are currently making — projects, deliverables, relationships, presences, performances. For each, mark honestly whether it is ripe, not yet ripe, or unsure. Then name what would make it ready, and what it is costing you to deliver it now.

THE OFFERING	RIPE	NOT YET	UNSURE	WHAT WOULD MAKE IT READY	WHAT IT IS COSTING ME TO DELIVER IT NOW

NOTES

ROTATE TO READ

SITTING WITH WHAT YOU FOUND

Now read your own inventory back. The pattern is what matters here, not any single line. What is the inventory telling you about how you are offering right now?

THE PATTERN

Of the offerings you listed, how many are ripe? How many are not? What does the ratio tell you?

____

____

____

THE COST

What are you actually losing when you deliver what is not ripe — not in the abstract, but specifically?

____

____

____

____

THE REPAIR

Which one offering, if you stopped delivering it before it was ready, would change the most? What would change?

____

____

____

____

____

____

____

____

____

____

____

PART TWO · CHAPTER TWO

COLLAPSED SACRED TIME

Sacred time is the time that does not produce. It withdraws, consolidates, restores. Without it, an arc cannot complete — only repeat. Collapsed sacred time is the most invisible of the timing wounds because it does not announce itself. It accumulates.

You may notice it first as fatigue that rest does not resolve, or as a feeling that the year has no shape — only continuous demand. Sacred time has not disappeared because you are lazy. It has disappeared because something has crowded it out, and the crowding has gone unexamined.

THE FOUR MARKS

Sacred time has collapsed in a domain when:

- Return has become indistinguishable from low-grade availability — you "rest" while still answering messages, planning, monitoring.

- The withdrawal that used to mark a season's end has been replaced by a brief decompression and a new beginning.

- You can no longer remember the last time you were not preparing for, executing, or recovering from a deliverable.

- The sacred days you once kept — sabbath, sabbat, retreat, fallow — have become workdays with different names.

What looks empty is preparing the next arc.
What is never allowed to be empty cannot prepare anything.

WHERE HAS RETURN GONE?

Map the structures of Return in your life — the daily, weekly, seasonal, and annual withdrawals. For each, name what it used to be, what it has become, and what specifically replaced it.

THE RETURN STRUCTURE	WHAT IT USED TO BE	WHAT IT IS NOW	WHAT REPLACED IT
Daily Return end of workday, sleep ritual, evening			
Weekly Return sabbath, day off, withdrawn day			
Seasonal Return retreat, fallow week, sabbat			
Annual Return fallow month, dark season, sabbatical			

ROTATE TO READ

● CHAPTER TWO · REFLECTION

WHAT IS ASKING TO BE REPAIRED

*You have audited what was lost. Now name what is asking to be restored —
not in the abstract, but as one specific structural change that could begin this
season.*

THE LOSS YOU FEEL MOST

*Which collapsed Return do you grieve most? Which one's absence do you feel daily,
even if you have stopped naming it?*

____

____

____

WHAT TOOK IT

*Sacred time does not vanish on its own. Something replaced it. Name what — without
justifying or rationalizing the replacement.*

____

____

____

____

● CHAPTER TWO · REFLECTION (CONTINUED)

THE SMALLEST HONEST REPAIR

Not the heroic restoration. The smallest, most honest repair you could begin this week. What would it be?

III

THE VIOLATION YOU'RE COMMITTING

Each season has a discipline, and each discipline has a specific violation when it is broken. The wound is not generic exhaustion. It is one of these four — and naming yours precisely is the beginning of repair.

● Violating Becoming

You are demanding visible output from something still hidden. You are taxing a seed for fruit. The work cannot ripen because it is being asked to perform before it has formed.

Diagnostic: What do you keep dragging into visibility before it is ready, because you cannot tolerate the patience the unformed thing requires?

● Violating Authority

You are holding what you should be releasing. You are governing past the point where governance was needed. The container has become the constraint — what stabilized the work now suffocates it.

Diagnostic: What are you still holding because you do not know what you would be without holding it — even though it is no longer asking to be held?

● Violating Offering

You are giving without a gate. The offering has no defined end — it has become continuous, and what was meant to be release has become depletion.

Diagnostic: Where in your life have you stopped knowing how to close a gate, because closing has come to feel like betrayal?

● Violating Return

You have entered Return but refuse to let it be Return. You rest while remaining

NAMING YOURS

Read the four diagnostics from the previous page. Notice which one moves something in you — discomfort, recognition, or the wish to look away. Then write here.

WHICH VIOLATION IS YOURS

Name it as specifically as you can. Where is it living? What is it taking? What does it look like in your daily life — not in the abstract, but in concrete moments and decisions?

PART TWO · CHAPTER FOUR

IV. THE SEASON YOU'RE ACTING FROM

Of all the questions in this workbook, this one is the hardest. Not because it is complex, but because it is direct.

Most people in the timing wound are acting from a season they are not actually in. You may be acting from Authority while in Return. Acting from Offering while in Becoming. Acting from Becoming while what is needed is governance.

The gap is rarely chosen. It is enforced — by economic necessity, social role, family system, professional identity. The season you are *asked* to act from is not always the season you are actually in, and the gap between them is where the timing wound lives.

THE "AS IF" DIAGNOSTIC

Four questions. Take the time you need with each one.

- *If no one were watching, no one expected anything, and your livelihood were not at stake — what season would your body and attention say you are in?*

- *What season are you currently performing for the people who depend on you?*

- *How long have you been performing it?*

- *What do you fear would happen if the gap between the two were named?*

THE GAP YOU ARE LIVING IN

Write what is true. Not what is solvable. Not what you have a plan for. Just what is true about the gap between the season you are in and the season you are acting from.

____

____

____

____

____

____

____

____

____

____

____

____

SYNTHESIS

NAMING THE WOUND

You have done four pieces of work. Each one has surfaced something different. Now bring them together. What is the specific shape of your timing wound — named in one sentence, in your own voice?

A good name is concrete, not abstract. It points to a specific season being violated, a specific offering being made wrongly, a specific Return being avoided. It does not describe burnout in general — it describes *your* wound in particular.

Examples (not yours, but to show the form)

"I am offering finished work from a body that is in Return, and I have been doing it for two years."

"I am performing Authority over a household that no longer needs governing, because I do not know who I am without the role."

"I cannot let Becoming be hidden — I keep dragging it into visibility before it is ready, because patience feels like loss."

MY WOUND, NAMED

Write your sentence. Rewrite it until it is specific. This sentence becomes the diagnostic input for everything in Part Three.

____

____

____

____

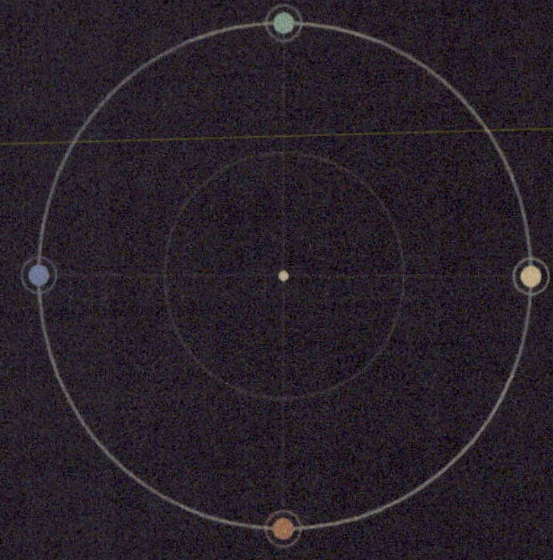

PART THREE

REPAIR TOOLS

Four instruments for closing the gap your self-assessment named. A rhythm rule. A gate. A constraint clause. A closing rite. None of them will repair the wound for you. All of them give you something to use when you choose to.

PART THREE · CHAPTER ONE

I THE RHYTHM RULE

A schedule fills time. A rhythm rule shapes it. The schedule says what you will do; the rhythm rule says how the day is allowed to breathe — when work is active, when withdrawal is sacred, where the gates between them sit.

You cannot repair a collapsed sacred time by adding rest to a full calendar. The rest will be the first thing canceled. What works instead is a rule about the shape of time itself — non-negotiable, pre-decided, structural. The rule does not require willpower in the moment, because the deciding has already happened.

WHAT A RHYTHM RULE IS NOT

- It is not a productivity system. It does not optimize your output.

- It is not a self-care routine. It does not "treat" you to rest as a reward.

- It is not flexible. The point of a rule is that it does not bend to the day's pressure.

The rule is what holds when willpower fails.
That is the entire reason it exists.

The next three pages help you build yours. First the structure of work and withdrawal. Then the daily, weekly, and seasonal cadence. Then the pressures that will challenge it — and what holds.

● CHAPTER ONE · DRAFTING

WORK MODE, WITHDRAWAL MODE

Begin with the two modes. What does it look like when you are genuinely working — engaged, producing, generative? What does it look like when you are genuinely withdrawn — unavailable, fallow, restoring? Name each as concretely as you can.

WHEN I AM IN WORK MODE

What does the day feel like? What am I doing, where, with what tools, with whom? What is the texture of attention?

____

____

____

____

WHEN I AM IN WITHDRAWAL MODE

What is true that is not true in work mode? What am I not doing? What is allowed to be slow, undecided, or absent?

____

____

____

____

MY RHYTHM RULE

Set the cadence. For each scale of time — daily, weekly, seasonal, annual — name when work is active, when withdrawal is sacred, and what marks the gate between. This is your rule. Write it short enough that you can hold it in your hand.

CADENCE	WORK MODE: WHEN, WHERE, WHAT SHAPE	WITHDRAWAL MODE: WHEN, WHERE, WHAT SHAPE	THE GATE BETWEEN THEM
Daily			
Weekly			
Seasonal			
Annual			

THE ONE-SENTENCE FORM OF MY RULE

ROTATE TO READ

● CHAPTER ONE · PRESSURE-TESTS

WHAT WILL CHALLENGE THE RULE

A rule that has never been tested is not yet a rule. Name the specific pressures that will come for yours — the requests, the anxieties, the patterns of others — and decide now what holds.

THE PRESSURES I CAN ALREADY SEE

Specific. "Work demands" is not specific. Which demands, from whom, at what time. "Anxiety" is not specific. The anxiety that asks me to check email at 9pm is.

____

____

____

WHAT I WILL SAY WHEN THE PRESSURE COMES

Predeclare the response. A sentence, written here, that you can reach for when the request arrives.

____

____

____

II

PART THREE · CHAPTER TWO

THE GATE

Every offering needs a gate. A gate is the structural mark of this offering is complete — without one, the offering becomes continuous, and Offering season becomes the only season you ever inhabit.

A real gate has three parts: it **opens** the offering deliberately, it **closes** it deliberately, and it **marks** the closure so that everyone — you first — knows the offering has ended. Without all three, the offering bleeds. People keep asking for it. You keep giving it. The fallow that should follow never arrives.

WHAT MAKES A GATE REAL

- **It is visible to others.** A private intention is not a gate. A public mark is.

- **It has a specific moment.** "When the project is done" is not a gate. "Friday at 5pm" is.

- **It has a closing act.** Something is sent, sealed, said, or marked. The closing leaves a trace.

- **It defends what follows.** The gate is the structure that protects the fallow on the other side.

A gate is not a wall.
It is what makes the difference between offering and bleeding.

BUILD YOUR GATES

List the offerings that need gates. For each, define how it opens, how it closes, and what marks the closure publicly. If you cannot name all three, the gate is not yet real.

THE OFFERING	HOW IT OPENS	HOW IT CLOSES	WHAT MARKS THE CLOSURE

NOTES

ROTATE TO READ

● CHAPTER TWO · TEMPLATES

THREE GATES TO ADOPT

Three common gates, sketched as templates. Adapt one or all to your life. The point is not the specific form — it is that the gate has a clear opening, closing, and mark.

The Work-Day Gate

Opens: at a set time, with a small starting act — a cup of tea, a written intention, opening the work file.

Closes: at a set time, before sunset where possible. Phone and email closed.

Marks: a written line in a notebook — *"Today I completed ___ . Tomorrow I will begin with ___ ."* The notebook goes to a defined place. The day is over.

The Project Gate

Opens: with a defined start — a kickoff, a first deliverable, a contract, a public announcement.

Closes: with a defined end date. Not "when it's done" but a date held in advance, communicated to others.

Marks: a closing communication that says explicitly: *this project is complete.* A note sent. A meeting held. A file archived. Followed by at least one week before the next project begins.

The Relationship Gate

Opens: with arrival — your full presence, attention given without distraction.

Closes: with departure — said clearly. *"I have to go now. I'll see you ___ ."* Not slipped away from.

Marks: the closing is named. The next contact is named. What was offered in this encounter is allowed to be enough.

III

PART THREE · CHAPTER THREE

THE CONSTRAINT CLAUSE

A constraint clause is a sentence you write before the pressure arrives. It declares, in advance, what you will and will not do when the demand rises. The point is to take the decision out of the moment — because in the moment, you will almost always say yes.

You named one version of this in Part One's Wheel Plan. This page sharpens it. The clause is not a list of rules. It is a single sentence, written in your own voice, that you can recite to yourself or to someone else when constraint increases. It works because it is decided, not negotiated.

WHAT A GOOD CLAUSE HAS

- **A specific trigger.** What kind of pressure activates it.

- **A specific action.** What you do (or do not do) in response.

- **A specific protection.** What the clause is defending — what would be lost without it.

Examples of the form:

"When my workload exceeds what one focused workday can hold, I will release the lowest-priority commitment rather than work after dark."

"When pressure rises, I will tighten existing gates before I consider opening new offerings."

"When I am being asked to be available outside my work hours, my first answer is no, and that answer holds for forty-eight hours."

● CHAPTER THREE · DRAFTING

DRAFTING YOUR CLAUSE

Write a draft. Read it back. Rewrite it. The clause is finished when it is specific enough to act on, and short enough to remember.

THE TRIGGER

What is the specific pressure your clause is for? When does it activate?

____

____

____

THE ACTION

What will you do — or refuse to do — when the trigger arrives?

____

____

____

THE PROTECTION

What does this clause defend? What would be lost if you did not have it?

____

____

____

IV

THE CLOSING RITE & VOW

The Closing Rite is the central repair structure of this work. It is what allows an arc to end — and therefore what allows a new one to begin. Without the rite, arcs do not close; they fade, and the fading is what becomes the timing wound.

The rite has two parts. The **Closing Rite** names and releases what is ending — the offering, the season, the identity, the role. The **Vow** names what you are committing to in what comes next, as a structural promise. The two together mark a real threshold: "this arc is complete, and another is beginning."

WHEN TO USE IT

- At the end of a significant offering — a book, a project, a season of caregiving.

- At the sabbat turning points — eight times a year, the Wheel itself asks for closing.

- When you notice an arc has already ended but you have not yet marked it.

- Whenever the gap between the season you are in and the season you are acting from grows too wide to bear.

The next two pages help you draft both parts. The page after that is a printable card — the Rite and Vow set in a form you can tear out, post near your work, and return to.

● CHAPTER FOUR · THE RITE

DRAFTING THE CLOSING RITE

Name what is ending. Name it concretely — not "this hard year" but this specific offering, this specific role, this specific season. The rite works because the closing is specific.

WHAT IS ENDING

The specific arc you are closing. What it was, when it began, what it asked of you.

____

____

____

____

WHAT I RELEASE

What goes with it. What duties, expectations, identities, tools, or beliefs are being set down.

____

____

____

____

● CHAPTER FOUR · THE RITE (CONTINUED)

THE CLOSING ACT

What you will do to mark the closing — written word, spoken sentence, object set aside, place visited, message sent. The act makes the closing real.

● CHAPTER FOUR · THE VOW

DRAFTING THE VOW

Name what begins. Not an aspiration. A structural promise — what you are committing to do or not do in the arc ahead. Specific. Defensible. Yours.

WHAT BEGINS

What is the shape of the next arc, as you can name it now? Not the full picture. Just the next true step.

____

____

____

WHAT I VOW

One or two specific commitments. Phrased as "I will..." or "I will not..." — concrete, not aspirational.

____

____

____

● CHAPTER FOUR · THE VOW (CONTINUED)

THE OPENING ACT

What you will do to mark the beginning. A first small step, taken in the open, that makes the new arc real.

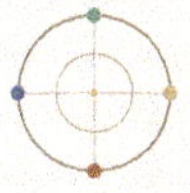

THE CLOSING RITE

What I now close

____

____

____

What I release with it

____

____

____

THE VOW

What I now begin

____

____

What I vow

CARRYING IT FORWARD

You have built four instruments — a rhythm rule, a gate, a clause, a closing rite. None of them will work on their own. They work when used, returned to, and revised.

The year-long journal that follows is where the using happens. Each week, your rhythm rule will be tested. Each offering, your gates will hold or fail. At each sabbat, the closing rite will ask to be performed — or refused. The journal is where you keep the record of which.

Before You Turn The Page

Take a moment to read back through what you have written across Parts Two and Three. Notice what has shifted in how you see your timing. Notice what you have committed to. Notice what remains uncertain, and let the uncertainty stay — the work of the year is to live the questions, not to solve them.

The Wheel turns. You are not asked to make it turn.
You are asked to recognize where in its turning you are.

Part Four begins on the next page.

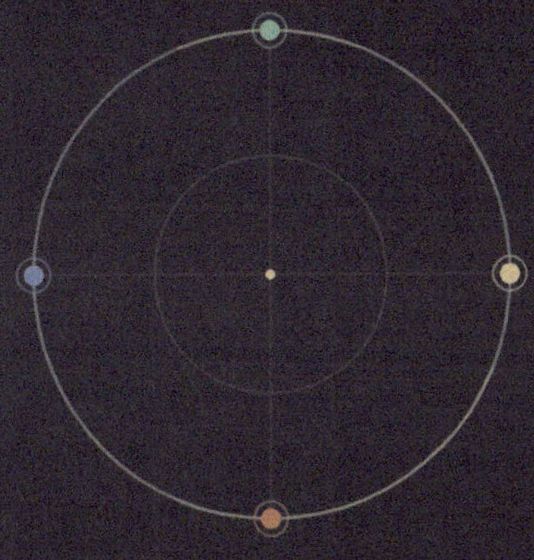

THE YEAR

Fifty-two weekly pages, eight sabbat thresholds, four quarterly reviews, and a year-end integration. This is where the tools you built in Part Three live across an actual year — used, tested, revised, returned to.

INSTRUCTIONS

HOW TO USE THIS JOURNAL

The journal is undated. You begin where you are. Each week, you fill in one ledger page — five minutes, longer if you have it. Every fourth week, the ledger asks a wider question. At each sabbat, you turn to the threshold page. At each quarter's end, you mark the broader pattern. At year's end, you integrate.

WEEKLY WHEEL LEDGER

Fill in the dates. Mark the days the rhythm rule held. Write what you offered and whether each had a gate. Note what Return looked like — even if it was absent. Note what pressed against the rule, and what held. End with one sentence: the truth of the week.

PATTERN CHECK

Every fourth week, the standard ledger gives way to a Pattern Check — the same frame, asking a wider question. What is the shape of the last four weeks? Where did Return land, and where did it not? What pressure recurred? The Pattern Check exists because a week is too short a window to see a wound; four weeks is sometimes enough.

SABBAT MARKERS AND THRESHOLDS

Eight times a year, the Wheel turns. Sabbat markers appear inline near the weeks where each sabbat sits in the calendar — small pointers to the full threshold pages at the back of Part Four. If your year is moving with the calendar, the marker arrives when the sabbat does. If you began the journal mid-year, the markers will not line up with your seasons; use the threshold pages directly when the turning is yours.

AN EXAMPLE WEEK

DATES   *April 28 – May 4*

The rhythm rule held on these days

OFFERINGS MADE THIS WEEK — AND WHETHER EACH HAD A GATE

Submitted the Q2 strategy doc Monday — closed the gate Tuesday with a hand-off email. Two student conferences (both finished cleanly). The newsletter went out Wednesday without a gate — I am still writing the next one in my head.

WITHDRAWAL — WHAT RETURN LOOKED LIKE, IF IT CAME AT ALL

Sunday afternoon protected — three hours, phone off, walked. No weekly Return otherwise. Thursday evening I sat down intending to rest and ended up answering work messages.

PRESSURE — WHAT TESTED THE RULE, AND WHAT HELD

A late request from the dean Friday afternoon to add a committee. I said yes in the room, then wrote back Saturday morning to retract. The clause held — barely.

THE TRUTH OF THE WEEK, IN ONE SENTENCE

I am offering steadily, but the gate is still not consistent. Next week: close the Thursday gate without negotiation.

WEEK 1

DATES

____

○ ○ ○ ○ ○ ○ ○
S M T W T F S

The rhythm rule held on these days

OFFERINGS MADE THIS WEEK — AND WHETHER EACH HAD A GATE

____

____

____

WITHDRAWAL — WHAT RETURN LOOKED LIKE, IF IT CAME AT ALL

____

____

____

PRESSURE — WHAT TESTED THE RULE, AND WHAT HELD

____

____

____

THE TRUTH OF THE WEEK, IN ONE SENTENCE

____

WEEK 2

DATES

____

O O O O O O O
S M T W T F S

____

The rhythm rule held on these days

OFFERINGS MADE THIS WEEK — AND WHETHER EACH HAD A GATE

____

____

____

WITHDRAWAL — WHAT RETURN LOOKED LIKE, IF IT CAME AT ALL

____

____

____

PRESSURE — WHAT TESTED THE RULE, AND WHAT HELD

____

____

____

THE TRUTH OF THE WEEK, IN ONE SENTENCE

____

WEEK 3

DATES

____

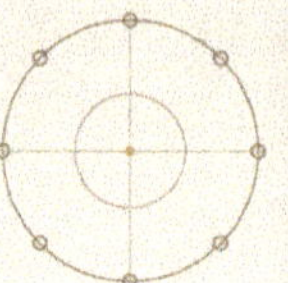

 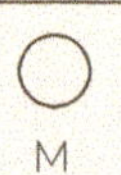 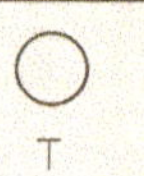 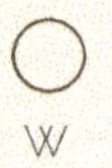  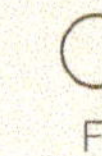 

S　　M　　T　　W　　T　　F　　S

The rhythm rule held on these days

OFFERINGS MADE THIS WEEK — AND WHETHER EACH HAD A GATE

____

____

____

WITHDRAWAL — WHAT RETURN LOOKED LIKE, IF IT CAME AT ALL

____

____

____

PRESSURE — WHAT TESTED THE RULE, AND WHAT HELD

____

____

____

THE TRUTH OF THE WEEK, IN ONE SENTENCE

____

WEEK 4

DATES

____

◯ ◯ ◯ ◯ ◯ ◯ ◯
S   M   T   W   T   F   S

The rhythm rule held on these days

THE SHAPE OF THE LAST FOUR WEEKS

____

____

____

WHERE RETURN LANDED, AND WHERE IT DID NOT

____

____

____

THE PRESSURE THAT RECURRED

____

____

____

WHAT THE FOUR WEEKS TOGETHER ARE SAYING, IN ONE SENTENCE

____

WEEK 5

DATES

____

◯ ◯ ◯ ◯ ◯ ◯ ◯
S   M   T   W   T   F   S

The rhythm rule held on these days

OFFERINGS MADE THIS WEEK — AND WHETHER EACH HAD A GATE

____

____

____

WITHDRAWAL — WHAT RETURN LOOKED LIKE, IF IT CAME AT ALL

____

____

____

PRESSURE — WHAT TESTED THE RULE, AND WHAT HELD

____

____

____

THE TRUTH OF THE WEEK, IN ONE SENTENCE

____

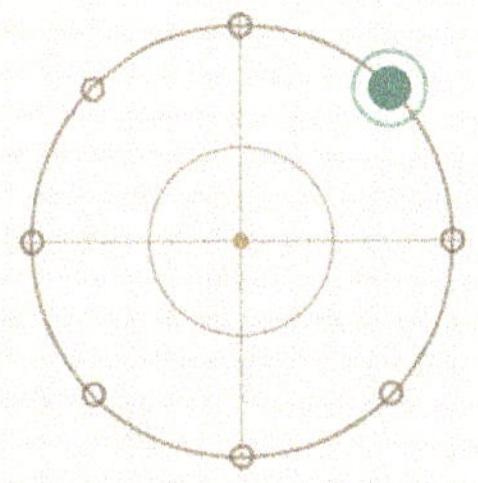

IMBOLC

If your year is moving with the calendar, Imbolc is near. Turn to the threshold page for Imbolc on page 123, then return to the ledger.

THRESHOLD · PAGE 123

IMBOLC

Cross-quarter · February 1

First stirring · Promise without proof · Strength as steadiness · Protection of what forms

WHEN

February 1 to sundown February 2. The cross-quarter between Yule and Ostara — halfway from winter solstice to spring equinox. The light has been lengthening since Yule, but here the change first becomes felt rather than only counted.

WHAT IT MARKS

The name comes from the Old Irish *i mbolc,* "in the belly." Imbolc marks the lambing season — the first signs of life returning to a still-frozen ground. The traditional Celtic first day of spring. The hearth fire kept burning through winter receives its first acknowledgement that it has been enough.

TRADITIONAL OBSERVANCE

Associated with Brigid: goddess of the forge, the hearth, poetry, and healing wells. Traditional observances include the lighting of candles, the making of Brigid's crosses from rushes, and the leaving of cloth on Brigid's eve to receive her blessing. Christianized as Candlemas. Folk practices emphasize purification, the cleaning of the hearth, and the first naming of what one intends to protect through the season ahead.

THE GOD'S ARC AT IMBOLC

At Imbolc, the God is the Uncrowned Heir. His light has returned since Yule — the direction of the year has shifted — and yet nothing in the visible world confirms his presence. The ground remains hard. Growth is not evident. He exists before he is convincing.

WHAT THE SEASON ASKS

Becoming asks for viability, not visibility. What is forming must be protected from the demand for immediate clarity, immediate output, immediate proof. The discipline of Imbolc is restraint — the decision to protect what is forming from a world that only knows how to harvest.

WEEK 6

DATES

____

O O O O O O O
S M T W T F S

The rhythm rule held on these days

OFFERINGS MADE THIS WEEK — AND WHETHER EACH HAD A GATE

____

____

____

WITHDRAWAL — WHAT RETURN LOOKED LIKE, IF IT CAME AT ALL

____

____

____

PRESSURE — WHAT TESTED THE RULE, AND WHAT HELD

____

____

THE TRUTH OF THE WEEK, IN ONE SENTENCE

____

WEEK 7

DATES

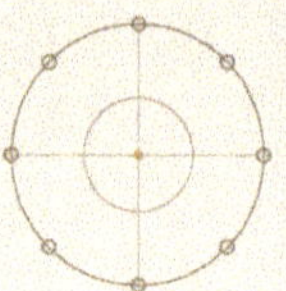

____

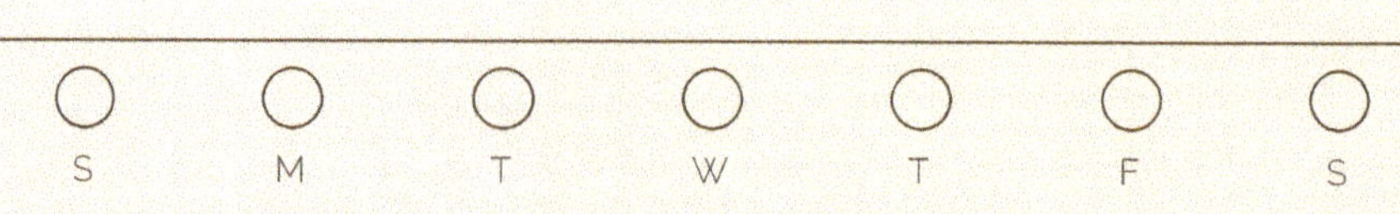

S   M   T   W   T   F   S

The rhythm rule held on these days

OFFERINGS MADE THIS WEEK — AND WHETHER EACH HAD A GATE

____

____

____

WITHDRAWAL — WHAT RETURN LOOKED LIKE, IF IT CAME AT ALL

____

____

____

PRESSURE — WHAT TESTED THE RULE, AND WHAT HELD

____

____

____

THE TRUTH OF THE WEEK, IN ONE SENTENCE

____

PATTERN CHECK · WEEKS 5 – 8

WEEK 8

DATES

S   M   T   W   T   F   S

The rhythm rule held on these days

THE SHAPE OF THE LAST FOUR WEEKS

WHERE RETURN LANDED, AND WHERE IT DID NOT

THE PRESSURE THAT RECURRED

WHAT THE FOUR WEEKS TOGETHER ARE SAYING, IN ONE SENTENCE

WEEK 9

DATES

____

◯ ◯ ◯ ◯ ◯ ◯ ◯
S   M   T   W   T   F   S

The rhythm rule held on these days

OFFERINGS MADE THIS WEEK — AND WHETHER EACH HAD A GATE

____

____

____

WITHDRAWAL — WHAT RETURN LOOKED LIKE, IF IT CAME AT ALL

____

____

____

PRESSURE — WHAT TESTED THE RULE, AND WHAT HELD

____

____

THE TRUTH OF THE WEEK, IN ONE SENTENCE

____

WEEK 10

DATES

____

S   M   T   W   T   F   S

The rhythm rule held on these days

OFFERINGS MADE THIS WEEK — AND WHETHER EACH HAD A GATE

____

____

____

WITHDRAWAL — WHAT RETURN LOOKED LIKE, IF IT CAME AT ALL

____

____

____

PRESSURE — WHAT TESTED THE RULE, AND WHAT HELD

____

____

THE TRUTH OF THE WEEK, IN ONE SENTENCE

____

WEEK 11

DATES

____

○   ○   ○   ○   ○   ○   ○
S   M   T   W   T   F   S

The rhythm rule held on these days

OFFERINGS MADE THIS WEEK — AND WHETHER EACH HAD A
GATE

____

____

____

WITHDRAWAL — WHAT RETURN LOOKED LIKE, IF IT CAME AT
ALL

____

____

____

PRESSURE — WHAT TESTED THE RULE, AND WHAT HELD

____

____

____

THE TRUTH OF THE WEEK, IN ONE SENTENCE

____

PATTERN CHECK · WEEKS 9 – 12

WEEK 12

DATES

S   M   T   W   T   F   S

The rhythm rule held on these days

THE SHAPE OF THE LAST FOUR WEEKS

WHERE RETURN LANDED, AND WHERE IT DID NOT

THE PRESSURE THAT RECURRED

WHAT THE FOUR WEEKS TOGETHER ARE SAYING, IN ONE SENTENCE

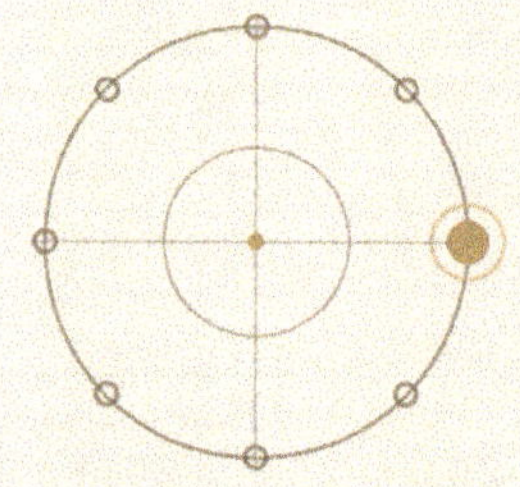

SABBAT IS NEAR

OSTARA

If your year is moving with the calendar, Ostara is near. Turn to the threshold page for Ostara on page 124, then return to the ledger.

THRESHOLD · PAGE 124

BECOMING

OSTARA

Spring equinox · on or near March 20

Rising into form · First contact with the world · Balance at the threshold · Becoming made visible

WHEN

On or near March 20 — the spring equinox, when day and night are equal and the light has begun visibly to win. One of the four solar holidays anchored to an astronomical event. The first of the Wheel's two equinoxes.

WHAT IT MARKS

What was forming underground at Imbolc now begins to disclose itself above the soil. Trees bud. Migratory animals return. The form is still forming — but it has begun to be visible. Ostara is the first moment when Becoming has something to show, and the first moment when that visibility becomes its own risk.

TRADITIONAL OBSERVANCE

The name is reconstructed from *Ēostre*, a Germanic dawn goddess attested by Bede. The Anglo-Saxon month *Ēosturmōnaþ* gives English "Easter." Traditional associations include hares, eggs, and seeds — symbols of latent life made visible. Folk practices: planting, blessing of seeds, ritual cleaning, the first walks on uncovered ground.

THE GOD'S ARC AT OSTARA

Ostara is the spring equinox — the moment when light and dark are briefly equal, and the world begins its outward turn. What was forming in the dark at Imbolc begins to surface. The Becoming is no longer only interior. It is now an object the world can see, name, and ask things of.

WHAT THE SEASON ASKS

A disclosed Becoming still belongs to the Becoming season. The form is not yet finished, and visibility is not the same as readiness. Those who can see what you are making do not get to set the timing of when it is ready.

WEEK 13

DATES _______________________________________

○   ○   ○   ○   ○   ○   ○

S   M   T   W   T   F   S

The rhythm rule held on these days

OFFERINGS MADE THIS WEEK — AND WHETHER EACH HAD A GATE

____

____

____

WITHDRAWAL — WHAT RETURN LOOKED LIKE, IF IT CAME AT ALL

____

____

____

PRESSURE — WHAT TESTED THE RULE, AND WHAT HELD

____

____

____

THE TRUTH OF THE WEEK, IN ONE SENTENCE

____

WEEK 14

DATES

____

O · O · O · O · O · O · O
S   M   T   W   T   F   S

The rhythm rule held on these days

OFFERINGS MADE THIS WEEK — AND WHETHER EACH HAD A GATE

____

____

____

WITHDRAWAL — WHAT RETURN LOOKED LIKE, IF IT CAME AT ALL

____

____

____

PRESSURE — WHAT TESTED THE RULE, AND WHAT HELD

____

____

THE TRUTH OF THE WEEK, IN ONE SENTENCE

____

WEEK 15

DATES

____

○ ○ ○ ○ ○ ○ ○
S M T W T F S

The rhythm rule held on these days

OFFERINGS MADE THIS WEEK — AND WHETHER EACH HAD A GATE

____

____

____

WITHDRAWAL — WHAT RETURN LOOKED LIKE, IF IT CAME AT ALL

____

____

____

PRESSURE — WHAT TESTED THE RULE, AND WHAT HELD

____

____

____

THE TRUTH OF THE WEEK, IN ONE SENTENCE

____

PATTERN CHECK · WEEKS 13 – 16

WEEK 16

DATES

S   M   T   W   T   F   S

The rhythm rule held on these days

THE SHAPE OF THE LAST FOUR WEEKS

WHERE RETURN LANDED, AND WHERE IT DID NOT

THE PRESSURE THAT RECURRED

WHAT THE FOUR WEEKS TOGETHER ARE SAYING, IN ONE SENTENCE

WEEK 17

DATES

____

○ ○ ○ ○ ○ ○ ○
S   M   T   W   T   F   S

The rhythm rule held on these days

OFFERINGS MADE THIS WEEK — AND WHETHER EACH HAD A
GATE

____

____

____

WITHDRAWAL — WHAT RETURN LOOKED LIKE, IF IT CAME AT
ALL

____

____

____

PRESSURE — WHAT TESTED THE RULE, AND WHAT HELD

____

____

____

THE TRUTH OF THE WEEK, IN ONE SENTENCE

____

WEEK 18

DATES

____

◯ ◯ ◯ ◯ ◯ ◯ ◯
S   M   T   W   T   F   S

The rhythm rule held on these days

OFFERINGS MADE THIS WEEK — AND WHETHER EACH HAD A GATE

____

____

____

WITHDRAWAL — WHAT RETURN LOOKED LIKE, IF IT CAME AT ALL

____

____

____

PRESSURE — WHAT TESTED THE RULE, AND WHAT HELD

____

____

____

THE TRUTH OF THE WEEK, IN ONE SENTENCE

____

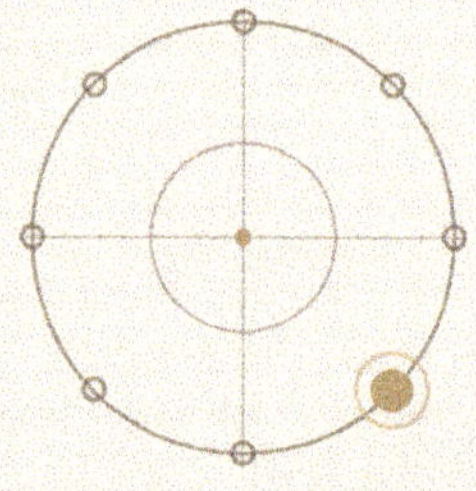

Beltane

If your year is moving with the calendar, Beltane is near. Turn to the threshold page for Beltane on page 125, then return to the ledger.

THRESHOLD · PAGE 125

AUTHORITY

BELTANE

Cross-quarter · May 1

Fire and the proof of form · Continuity within heat · Boundary discovered, not imposed · The intensity that tests

WHEN

May 1 — the cross-quarter between Ostara and Litha, halfway from the spring equinox to the summer solstice. Some traditions begin the observance at sundown April 30 (May Eve). The opening of the bright half of the year in the Celtic calendar.

WHAT IT MARKS

What has formed since Imbolc is now under heat. Beltane is where the year asks whether what came into form can hold its form under intensity. Cattle were traditionally driven between two bonfires to bless and protect them before being moved to summer pasture — a passage through fire that proves what can pass through it.

TRADITIONAL OBSERVANCE

From Old Irish *Beltaine*, often glossed as "bright fire." Associated with the god Belenus and with sovereignty figures across the Celtic world. Traditional observances include the lighting of twin bonfires, the dancing of the maypole, the gathering of May dew, and rites that mark the meeting of complementary powers. A fire festival paired across the year with Samhain.

THE GOD'S ARC AT BELTANE

Beltane is not a festival. It is the season's testing of form. What has formed is asked whether it can survive intensity without dissolving — whether the boundary it has discovered can hold while everything in the field presses toward the dissolution of coherence. This is the proof of form.

WHAT THE SEASON ASKS

The boundary at Beltane is not restriction. Restriction is imposed from outside. Boundary is discovered, integrated, and maintained as the form of genuine engagement. What holds its form under heat has boundary that is adequate to the conditions. What does not, learns where the form is still forming.

WEEK 19

DATES

____

◯   ◯   ◯   ◯   ◯   ◯   ◯
S   M   T   W   T   F   S

The rhythm rule held on these days

OFFERINGS MADE THIS WEEK — AND WHETHER EACH HAD A GATE

____

____

____

WITHDRAWAL — WHAT RETURN LOOKED LIKE, IF IT CAME AT ALL

____

____

____

PRESSURE — WHAT TESTED THE RULE, AND WHAT HELD

____

____

____

THE TRUTH OF THE WEEK, IN ONE SENTENCE

____

PATTERN CHECK · WEEKS 17 – 20

WEEK 20

DATES

—————————————————————————————

○ ○ ○ ○ ○ ○ ○

S　M　T　W　T　F　S

The rhythm rule held on these days

THE SHAPE OF THE LAST FOUR WEEKS

—————————————————————————————

—————————————————————————————

—————————————————————————————

WHERE RETURN LANDED, AND WHERE IT DID NOT

—————————————————————————————

—————————————————————————————

—————————————————————————————

THE PRESSURE THAT RECURRED

—————————————————————————————

—————————————————————————————

—————————————————————————————

WHAT THE FOUR WEEKS TOGETHER ARE SAYING, IN ONE SENTENCE

—————————————————————————————

WEEK 21

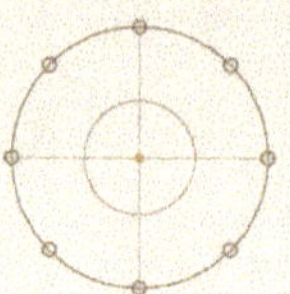

DATES

____

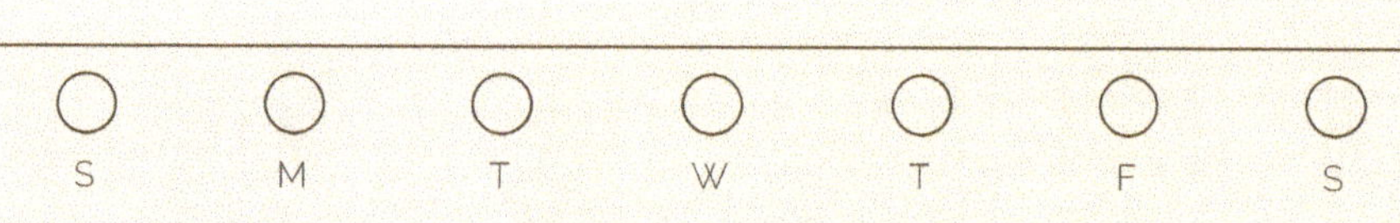

○ ○ ○ ○ ○ ○ ○
S M T W T F S

The rhythm rule held on these days

OFFERINGS MADE THIS WEEK — AND WHETHER EACH HAD A GATE

____

____

WITHDRAWAL — WHAT RETURN LOOKED LIKE, IF IT CAME AT ALL

____

____

____

PRESSURE — WHAT TESTED THE RULE, AND WHAT HELD

____

____

____

THE TRUTH OF THE WEEK, IN ONE SENTENCE

____

WEEK 22

DATES

____

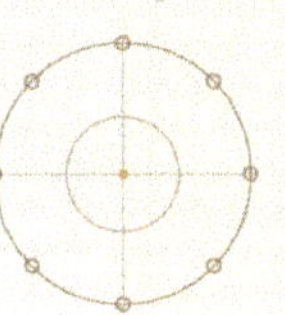

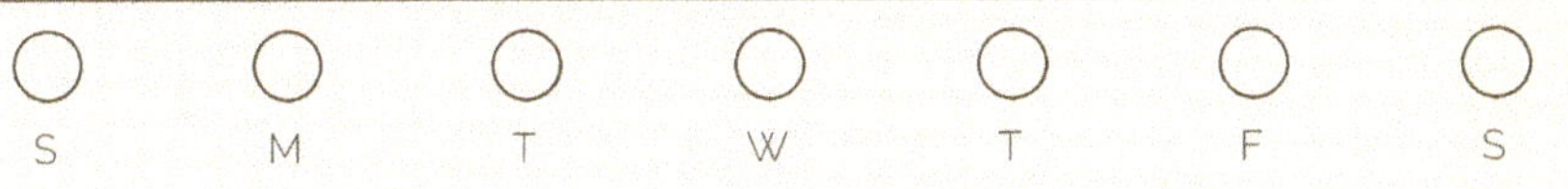

S   M   T   W   T   F   S

The rhythm rule held on these days

OFFERINGS MADE THIS WEEK — AND WHETHER EACH HAD A GATE

____

____

____

WITHDRAWAL — WHAT RETURN LOOKED LIKE, IF IT CAME AT ALL

____

____

____

PRESSURE — WHAT TESTED THE RULE, AND WHAT HELD

____

____

THE TRUTH OF THE WEEK, IN ONE SENTENCE

____

WEEK 23

DATES ____

____

◯ ◯ ◯ ◯ ◯ ◯ ◯
S M T W T F S

The rhythm rule held on these days

OFFERINGS MADE THIS WEEK — AND WHETHER EACH HAD A GATE

____

____

____

WITHDRAWAL — WHAT RETURN LOOKED LIKE, IF IT CAME AT ALL

____

____

____

PRESSURE — WHAT TESTED THE RULE, AND WHAT HELD

____

____

____

THE TRUTH OF THE WEEK, IN ONE SENTENCE

____

PATTERN CHECK · WEEKS 21 – 24

WEEK 24

DATES

____

◯ ◯ ◯ ◯ ◯ ◯ ◯
S   M   T   W   T   F   S

The rhythm rule held on these days

THE SHAPE OF THE LAST FOUR WEEKS

____

____

____

WHERE RETURN LANDED, AND WHERE IT DID NOT

____

____

____

THE PRESSURE THAT RECURRED

____

____

____

WHAT THE FOUR WEEKS TOGETHER ARE SAYING, IN ONE SENTENCE

____

WEEK 25

DATES

____

○   ○   ○   ○   ○   ○   ○
S   M   T   W   T   F   S

The rhythm rule held on these days

OFFERINGS MADE THIS WEEK — AND WHETHER EACH HAD A
GATE

____

____

WITHDRAWAL — WHAT RETURN LOOKED LIKE, IF IT CAME AT
ALL

____

____

PRESSURE — WHAT TESTED THE RULE, AND WHAT HELD

____

____

THE TRUTH OF THE WEEK, IN ONE SENTENCE

____

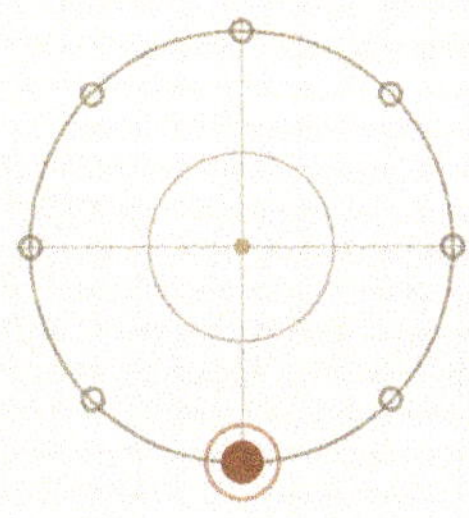

SABBAT IS NEAR

LITHA

If your year is moving with the calendar, Litha is near. Turn to the threshold page for Litha on page 126, then return to the ledger.

THRESHOLD · PAGE 126

AUTHORITY

LITHA

Summer solstice · on or near June 20

Full sovereignty · The crown is worn · Holding without permanence · The peak that already turns

WHEN

On or near June 20 — the summer solstice, the longest day and shortest night of the year. One of the four solar holidays. Also called Midsummer. The astronomical peak of solar power; from this day, the days begin to shorten.

WHAT IT MARKS

The height of Authority. The God is fully in his sovereignty — visible, sustained, ordered, protective of what depends on him. What was tested at Beltane has held, and what holds is now asked to govern. Crops are growing toward fullness. The work is steady. The territory is established.

TRADITIONAL OBSERVANCE

The name *Litha* is taken from Bede's Anglo-Saxon calendar, where it named the months around midsummer. Traditional European observances include solstice bonfires, the gathering of midsummer herbs (St. John's wort, vervain, mugwort) at peak potency, all-night vigils to greet the dawn, and rites honoring the height-of-the-year sun. Often paired across the wheel with Yule.

THE GOD'S ARC AT LITHA

Light reaches its height. The God is sovereign — visible, radiant, fully expressed. But even at the summit, Litha carries a whisper of turning. The longest day contains the knowledge that days will shorten. The crowned God does not say, "I am the crown." He says, "The crown is mine to carry for this season."

WHAT THE SEASON ASKS

The discipline of Litha is to hold power without believing it is permanent — to govern without confusing stewardship with identity. The peak is a passage. Staying at the peak past the peak is the structure of burnout.

WEEK 26

DATES

____

O   O   O   O   O   O   O
S   M   T   W   T   F   S

The rhythm rule held on these days

OFFERINGS MADE THIS WEEK — AND WHETHER EACH HAD A GATE

____

____

____

WITHDRAWAL — WHAT RETURN LOOKED LIKE, IF IT CAME AT ALL

____

____

____

PRESSURE — WHAT TESTED THE RULE, AND WHAT HELD

____

____

____

THE TRUTH OF THE WEEK, IN ONE SENTENCE

____

WEEK 27

DATES

____

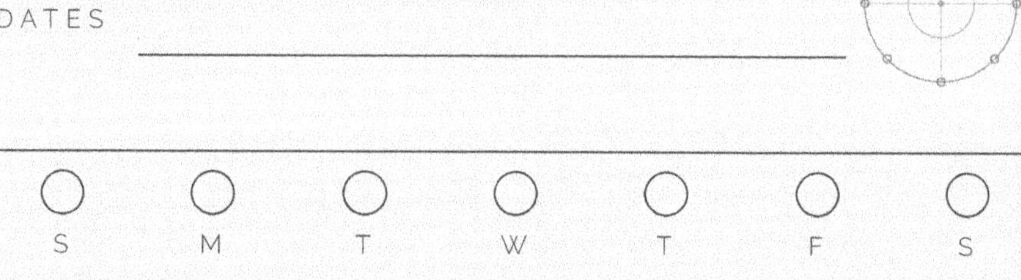

○ ○ ○ ○ ○ ○ ○

S M T W T F S

The rhythm rule held on these days

OFFERINGS MADE THIS WEEK — AND WHETHER EACH HAD A GATE

____

____

____

WITHDRAWAL — WHAT RETURN LOOKED LIKE, IF IT CAME AT ALL

____

____

____

PRESSURE — WHAT TESTED THE RULE, AND WHAT HELD

____

____

____

THE TRUTH OF THE WEEK, IN ONE SENTENCE

____

PATTERN CHECK · WEEKS 25 – 28

WEEK 28

DATES

S   M   T   W   T   F   S

The rhythm rule held on these days

THE SHAPE OF THE LAST FOUR WEEKS

WHERE RETURN LANDED, AND WHERE IT DID NOT

THE PRESSURE THAT RECURRED

WHAT THE FOUR WEEKS TOGETHER ARE SAYING, IN ONE SENTENCE

WEEK 29

DATES

____

◯   ◯   ◯   ◯   ◯   ◯   ◯
S   M   T   W   T   F   S

The rhythm rule held on these days

OFFERINGS MADE THIS WEEK — AND WHETHER EACH HAD A GATE

____

____

____

WITHDRAWAL — WHAT RETURN LOOKED LIKE, IF IT CAME AT ALL

____

____

____

PRESSURE — WHAT TESTED THE RULE, AND WHAT HELD

____

____

____

THE TRUTH OF THE WEEK, IN ONE SENTENCE

____

WEEK 30

DATES

S   M   T   W   T   F   S

The rhythm rule held on these days

OFFERINGS MADE THIS WEEK — AND WHETHER EACH HAD A GATE

WITHDRAWAL — WHAT RETURN LOOKED LIKE, IF IT CAME AT ALL

PRESSURE — WHAT TESTED THE RULE, AND WHAT HELD

THE TRUTH OF THE WEEK, IN ONE SENTENCE

WEEK 31

DATES

____

○   ○   ○   ○   ○   ○   ○

S   M   T   W   T   F   S

The rhythm rule held on these days

OFFERINGS MADE THIS WEEK — AND WHETHER EACH HAD A GATE

____

____

____

WITHDRAWAL — WHAT RETURN LOOKED LIKE, IF IT CAME AT ALL

____

____

____

PRESSURE — WHAT TESTED THE RULE, AND WHAT HELD

____

____

____

THE TRUTH OF THE WEEK, IN ONE SENTENCE

____

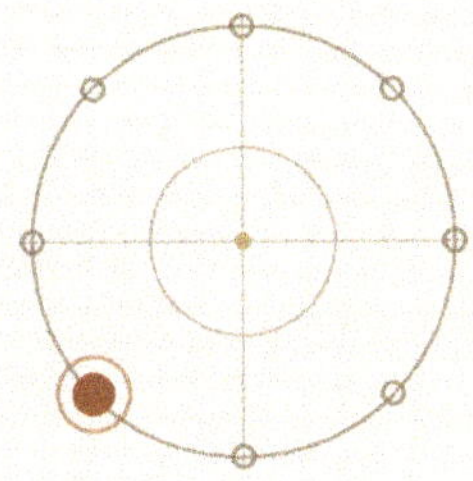

Lammas

If your year is moving with the calendar, Lammas is near. Turn to the threshold page for Lammas on page 127, then return to the ledger.

THRESHOLD · PAGE 127

LAMMAS

Cross-quarter · August 1

First harvest · Ripeness before release · Offering with a gate · Labor becomes sustenance

WHEN

August 1 — the cross-quarter between Litha and Mabon, halfway from summer solstice to autumn equinox. Also called Lughnasadh in the Irish tradition. The earliest of the three harvest sabbats.

WHAT IT MARKS

The first harvest. Specifically the grain harvest — wheat, barley, oats, cut and threshed. The growing has ended; the giving has begun. What has been held since Beltane is now beginning to be released. The God offers himself to the land for the first time in the year — not because the land demanded it endlessly, but because the season was ripe.

TRADITIONAL OBSERVANCE

From Old English *hlāfmæsse*, "loaf-mass" — the first bread from the year's new wheat was traditionally blessed. The Irish *Lughnasadh* is named for Lugh, who was said to have established the festival as funeral games for his foster-mother Tailtiu. Traditional observances include the baking of the first loaf, fairs and athletic games, the climbing of holy hills, and rites of first-fruits offering.

THE GOD'S ARC AT LAMMAS

At Lammas, the God offers from what has matured. He does not offer from the seed — he offers from the harvest. And the offering has a gate. He gives, and then he begins his descent. Right-timed offering circulates life. Mis-timed offering circulates exhaustion.

WHAT THE SEASON ASKS

If your giving has no gate, no season, no end, then what you are doing — however noble it feels — is not the God's offering. It is extraction wearing sacred clothing. Lammas asks for the naming of the gate at the beginning of the giving.

PATTERN CHECK · WEEKS 29 – 32

WEEK 32

DATES

S   M   T   W   T   F   S

The rhythm rule held on these days

THE SHAPE OF THE LAST FOUR WEEKS

WHERE RETURN LANDED, AND WHERE IT DID NOT

THE PRESSURE THAT RECURRED

WHAT THE FOUR WEEKS TOGETHER ARE SAYING, IN ONE
SENTENCE

WEEK 33

DATES

____

◯   ◯   ◯   ◯   ◯   ◯   ◯
S   M   T   W   T   F   S

The rhythm rule held on these days

OFFERINGS MADE THIS WEEK — AND WHETHER EACH HAD A GATE

____

____

____

WITHDRAWAL — WHAT RETURN LOOKED LIKE, IF IT CAME AT ALL

____

____

____

PRESSURE — WHAT TESTED THE RULE, AND WHAT HELD

____

____

____

THE TRUTH OF THE WEEK, IN ONE SENTENCE

____

WEEK 34

DATES

____

◯   ◯   ◯   ◯   ◯   ◯   ◯

S   M   T   W   T   F   S

The rhythm rule held on these days

OFFERINGS MADE THIS WEEK — AND WHETHER EACH HAD A GATE

____

____

____

WITHDRAWAL — WHAT RETURN LOOKED LIKE, IF IT CAME AT ALL

____

____

____

PRESSURE — WHAT TESTED THE RULE, AND WHAT HELD

____

____

____

THE TRUTH OF THE WEEK, IN ONE SENTENCE

____

WEEK 35

DATES

____

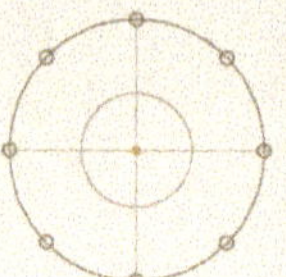

○ ○ ○ ○ ○ ○ ○

S   M   T   W   T   F   S

The rhythm rule held on these days

OFFERINGS MADE THIS WEEK — AND WHETHER EACH HAD A GATE

____

____

____

WITHDRAWAL — WHAT RETURN LOOKED LIKE, IF IT CAME AT ALL

____

____

____

PRESSURE — WHAT TESTED THE RULE, AND WHAT HELD

____

____

____

THE TRUTH OF THE WEEK, IN ONE SENTENCE

____

PATTERN CHECK · WEEKS 33 – 36

WEEK 36

DATES

S   M   T   W   T   F   S

The rhythm rule held on these days

THE SHAPE OF THE LAST FOUR WEEKS

WHERE RETURN LANDED, AND WHERE IT DID NOT

THE PRESSURE THAT RECURRED

WHAT THE FOUR WEEKS TOGETHER ARE SAYING, IN ONE SENTENCE

WEEK 37

DATES

____

◯ ◯ ◯ ◯ ◯ ◯ ◯

S   M   T   W   T   F   S

The rhythm rule held on these days

OFFERINGS MADE THIS WEEK — AND WHETHER EACH HAD A GATE

____

____

____

WITHDRAWAL — WHAT RETURN LOOKED LIKE, IF IT CAME AT ALL

____

____

____

PRESSURE — WHAT TESTED THE RULE, AND WHAT HELD

____

____

____

THE TRUTH OF THE WEEK, IN ONE SENTENCE

____

WEEK 38

DATES

____

◯ ◯ ◯ ◯ ◯ ◯ ◯
S   M   T   W   T   F   S

The rhythm rule held on these days

OFFERINGS MADE THIS WEEK — AND WHETHER EACH HAD A GATE

____

____

____

WITHDRAWAL — WHAT RETURN LOOKED LIKE, IF IT CAME AT ALL

____

____

____

PRESSURE — WHAT TESTED THE RULE, AND WHAT HELD

____

____

____

THE TRUTH OF THE WEEK, IN ONE SENTENCE

____

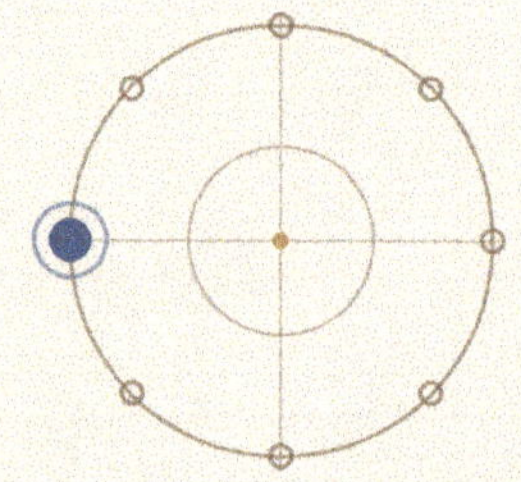

SABBAT IS NEAR

MABON

If your year is moving with the calendar, Mabon is near. Turn to the threshold page for Mabon on page 128, then return to the ledger.

THRESHOLD · PAGE 128

OFFERING

MABON

Autumn equinox · on or near September 22

Final harvest · Balance before descent · Completing the giving · The gate closes

WHEN

On or near September 22 — the autumn equinox, when day and night are equal and the light is visibly losing. One of the four solar holidays. The mirror of Ostara across the wheel.

WHAT IT MARKS

The middle of the harvest season. Fruits, vegetables, and late grains are at their peak. The year visibly turns from giving outward to drawing inward. The light has been declining since Litha; the dark has been gathering since the longest day. Mabon names the symmetry that has been true for months.

TRADITIONAL OBSERVANCE

The name *Mabon* was given to this sabbat by Aidan Kelly in the 1970s, taken from the Welsh figure Mabon ap Modron ("son of the mother") in the Mabinogion. Traditional European harvest observances include feasts of thanksgiving, the gathering and preservation of stores, the blessing of orchards and vines, and rites that mark the balance of dark and light.

THE GOD'S ARC AT MABON

Mabon marks the threshold into withdrawal. The final harvest is gathered. What can be given has been given. The Offering season does not end in scarcity — it ends in completion. Mabon asks you to recognize when the giving is genuinely finished, as fidelity to the arc.

WHAT THE SEASON ASKS

The gate of Offering closes here. What remains must be carried inward — preserved for what must survive the descent. The honesty of the equinox is the accounting: what has been given, what has been withheld, what is finished.

WEEK 39

DATES

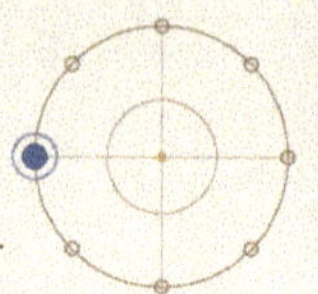

S M T W T F S

The rhythm rule held on these days

OFFERINGS MADE THIS WEEK — AND WHETHER EACH HAD A GATE

WITHDRAWAL — WHAT RETURN LOOKED LIKE, IF IT CAME AT ALL

PRESSURE — WHAT TESTED THE RULE, AND WHAT HELD

THE TRUTH OF THE WEEK, IN ONE SENTENCE

PATTERN CHECK · WEEKS 37 – 40

WEEK 40

DATES

____

○ ○ ○ ○ ○ ○ ○
S   M   T   W   T   F   S

The rhythm rule held on these days

THE SHAPE OF THE LAST FOUR WEEKS

____

____

____

WHERE RETURN LANDED, AND WHERE IT DID NOT

____

____

____

THE PRESSURE THAT RECURRED

____

____

____

WHAT THE FOUR WEEKS TOGETHER ARE SAYING, IN ONE
SENTENCE

____

WEEK 41

DATES ____

○   ○   ○   ○   ○   ○   ○
S   M   T   W   T   F   S

The rhythm rule held on these days

OFFERINGS MADE THIS WEEK — AND WHETHER EACH HAD A GATE

____

____

____

WITHDRAWAL — WHAT RETURN LOOKED LIKE, IF IT CAME AT ALL

____

____

____

PRESSURE — WHAT TESTED THE RULE, AND WHAT HELD

____

____

____

THE TRUTH OF THE WEEK, IN ONE SENTENCE

____

WEEK 42

DATES

____

○   ○   ○   ○   ○   ○   ○

S   M   T   W   T   F   S

The rhythm rule held on these days

OFFERINGS MADE THIS WEEK — AND WHETHER EACH HAD A GATE

____

____

____

WITHDRAWAL — WHAT RETURN LOOKED LIKE, IF IT CAME AT ALL

____

____

____

PRESSURE — WHAT TESTED THE RULE, AND WHAT HELD

____

____

____

THE TRUTH OF THE WEEK, IN ONE SENTENCE

____

WEEK 43

DATES

____

◯ ◯ ◯ ◯ ◯ ◯ ◯
S   M   T   W   T   F   S

The rhythm rule held on these days

OFFERINGS MADE THIS WEEK — AND WHETHER EACH HAD A GATE

____

____

____

WITHDRAWAL — WHAT RETURN LOOKED LIKE, IF IT CAME AT ALL

____

____

____

PRESSURE — WHAT TESTED THE RULE, AND WHAT HELD

____

____

____

THE TRUTH OF THE WEEK, IN ONE SENTENCE

____

PATTERN CHECK · WEEKS 41 – 44

WEEK 44

DATES

S   M   T   W   T   F   S

The rhythm rule held on these days

THE SHAPE OF THE LAST FOUR WEEKS

WHERE RETURN LANDED, AND WHERE IT DID NOT

THE PRESSURE THAT RECURRED

WHAT THE FOUR WEEKS TOGETHER ARE SAYING, IN ONE SENTENCE

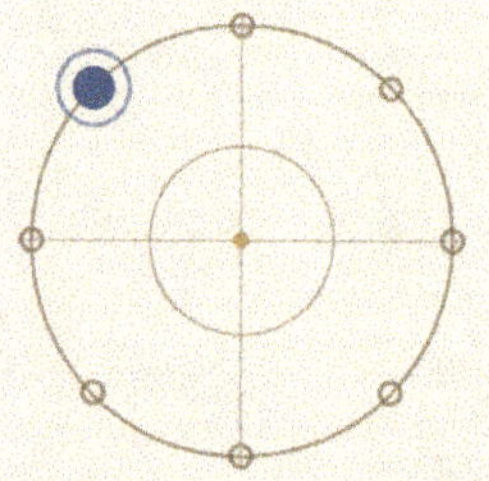

SAMHAIN

If your year is moving with the calendar, Samhain is near. Turn to the threshold page for Samhain on page 129, then return to the ledger.

THRESHOLD · PAGE 129

RETURN

SAMHAIN

Cross-quarter · October 31

Descent begins · Voluntary disappearance · The veil thins · Completion, not defeat

WHEN

October 31 to sundown November 1 — the cross-quarter between Mabon and Yule, halfway from autumn equinox to winter solstice. The traditional Celtic new year. The closing of the bright half of the year and the opening of the dark half.

WHAT IT MARKS

The final harvest. The slaughter of livestock that would not be kept through winter. The last gathering of stores. The threshold across which the year passes into fallow. In the Celtic tradition, the veil between the living and the dead is thinnest now.

TRADITIONAL OBSERVANCE

From Old Irish *Samain*, "summer's end." One of the two great Celtic fire festivals, paired with Beltane across the wheel. Traditional observances include bonfires kindled from the year's extinguished hearths, the setting of places for the dead at table, divination rites, and the wearing of disguises to move safely through the open threshold. Christianized as All Hallows.

THE GOD'S ARC AT SAMHAIN

At Samhain, the God relinquishes form. He has risen, reigned, offered, and now he descends. Authority is released. Life withdraws into memory and seed. The visible God becomes invisible — not destroyed, but concealed. He enters the dark not as defeat, but as completion of the arc.

WHAT THE SEASON ASKS

This is the image the modern world cannot tolerate: the voluntary disappearance of what was powerful. We understand loss. We understand failure. Voluntary descent — stepping back from visibility because the season requires it — feels like death to a world that equates existence with output. The Wheel turns regardless.

WEEK 45

DATES ____

S   M   T   W   T   F   S

The rhythm rule held on these days

OFFERINGS MADE THIS WEEK — AND WHETHER EACH HAD A GATE

____

____

____

WITHDRAWAL — WHAT RETURN LOOKED LIKE, IF IT CAME AT ALL

____

____

____

PRESSURE — WHAT TESTED THE RULE, AND WHAT HELD

____

____

____

THE TRUTH OF THE WEEK, IN ONE SENTENCE

____

WEEK 46

DATES

____

○ ○ ○ ○ ○ ○ ○
S   M   T   W   T   F   S

The rhythm rule held on these days

OFFERINGS MADE THIS WEEK — AND WHETHER EACH HAD A GATE

____

____

____

WITHDRAWAL — WHAT RETURN LOOKED LIKE, IF IT CAME AT ALL

____

____

____

PRESSURE — WHAT TESTED THE RULE, AND WHAT HELD

____

____

____

THE TRUTH OF THE WEEK, IN ONE SENTENCE

____

WEEK 47

DATES

____

○ ○ ○ ○ ○ ○ ○
S   M   T   W   T   F   S

The rhythm rule held on these days

OFFERINGS MADE THIS WEEK — AND WHETHER EACH HAD A GATE

____

____

____

WITHDRAWAL — WHAT RETURN LOOKED LIKE, IF IT CAME AT ALL

____

____

____

PRESSURE — WHAT TESTED THE RULE, AND WHAT HELD

____

____

____

THE TRUTH OF THE WEEK, IN ONE SENTENCE

____

PATTERN CHECK · WEEKS 45 – 48

WEEK 48

DATES

S   M   T   W   T   F   S

The rhythm rule held on these days

THE SHAPE OF THE LAST FOUR WEEKS

WHERE RETURN LANDED, AND WHERE IT DID NOT

THE PRESSURE THAT RECURRED

WHAT THE FOUR WEEKS TOGETHER ARE SAYING, IN ONE SENTENCE

WEEK 49

DATES

____

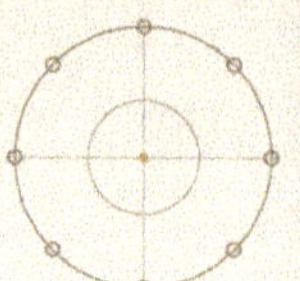

O   O   O   O   O   O   O

S   M   T   W   T   F   S

The rhythm rule held on these days

OFFERINGS MADE THIS WEEK — AND WHETHER EACH HAD A GATE

____

____

____

WITHDRAWAL — WHAT RETURN LOOKED LIKE, IF IT CAME AT ALL

____

____

____

PRESSURE — WHAT TESTED THE RULE, AND WHAT HELD

____

____

____

THE TRUTH OF THE WEEK, IN ONE SENTENCE

____

WEEK 50

DATES

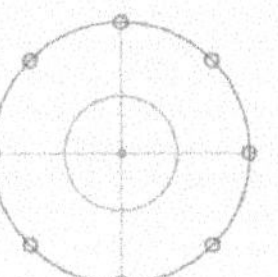

____

◯ ◯ ◯ ◯ ◯ ◯ ◯

S M T W T F S

The rhythm rule held on these days

OFFERINGS MADE THIS WEEK — AND WHETHER EACH HAD A GATE

____

____

____

WITHDRAWAL — WHAT RETURN LOOKED LIKE, IF IT CAME AT ALL

____

____

____

PRESSURE — WHAT TESTED THE RULE, AND WHAT HELD

____

____

____

THE TRUTH OF THE WEEK, IN ONE SENTENCE

____

WEEK 51

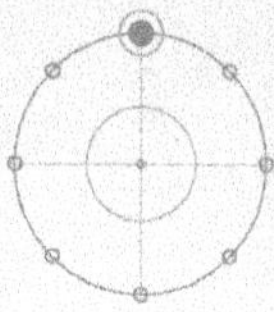

DATES ____

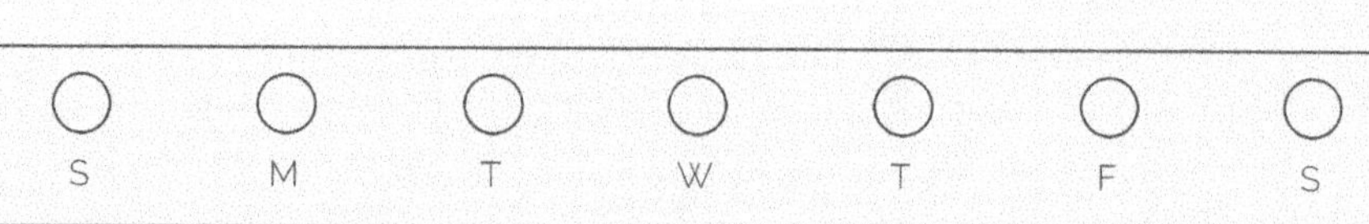

| S | M | T | W | T | F | S |

The rhythm rule held on these days

OFFERINGS MADE THIS WEEK — AND WHETHER EACH HAD A GATE

____

____

____

WITHDRAWAL — WHAT RETURN LOOKED LIKE, IF IT CAME AT ALL

____

____

____

PRESSURE — WHAT TESTED THE RULE, AND WHAT HELD

____

____

____

THE TRUTH OF THE WEEK, IN ONE SENTENCE

____

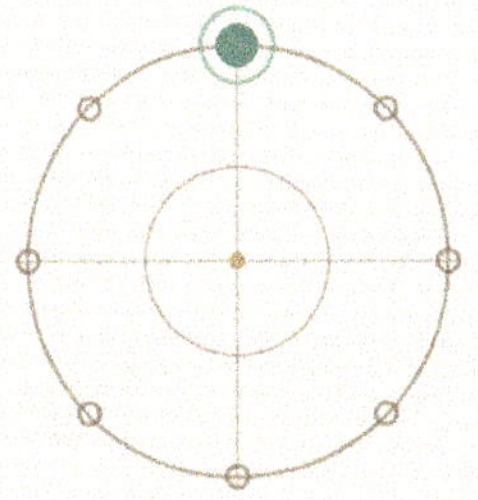

YULE

If your year is moving with the calendar, Yule is near. Turn to the threshold page for Yule on page 130, then return to the ledger.

THRESHOLD · PAGE 130

RETURN

YULE

Winter solstice · on or near December 21

Birth in darkness · The seed carried forward · Direction without confirmation · The turn that cannot be seen

WHEN

On or near December 21 — the winter solstice, the longest night and shortest day. One of the four solar holidays. The astronomical floor of solar power; from this day, the days begin to lengthen.

WHAT IT MARKS

The deepest point of the dark half of the year — and the threshold past which the return has begun. The seed sleeps. The fallow holds. Nothing yet asks to come back, but the turn has happened. The light that returns at Yule is not a reward. It is the consequence of a descent that was honored rather than refused.

TRADITIONAL OBSERVANCE

From Old Norse *jól* and Old English *geōl*, naming the midwinter feast attested across Germanic Europe. Traditional observances include the Yule log kindled from the previous year's remnant, evergreens brought into the house, all-night vigils to greet the returning sun at dawn, and feasts of preservation. Often paired across the wheel with Litha.

THE GOD'S ARC AT YULE

The God is born here — not crowned, not sovereign, not even fully formed. He is a direction. A signal. A seed of what will become. Yule belongs to Return because it is the dark that makes the next Becoming possible.

WHAT THE SEASON ASKS

Nothing yet asks to come back. The wound at Yule is the demand for emergence before the floor has been reached. Yule asks you to trust what cannot yet be demonstrated — to honor the descent the year has just completed before expecting the next forming to begin.

PATTERN CHECK · WEEKS 49 – 52

WEEK 52

DATES

____

◯   ◯   ◯   ◯   ◯   ◯   ◯

S   M   T   W   T   F   S

The rhythm rule held on these days

THE SHAPE OF THE LAST FOUR WEEKS

____

____

____

WHERE RETURN LANDED, AND WHERE IT DID NOT

____

____

____

THE PRESSURE THAT RECURRED

____

____

____

WHAT THE FOUR WEEKS TOGETHER ARE SAYING, IN ONE SENTENCE

____

IMBOLC

Imbolc is the first stirring of light after deep winter — the moment Becoming announces itself, hidden but no longer dormant. This sabbat asks you to notice what is forming in you that does not yet wish to be seen.

WHAT THIS SEASON IS ASKING

Name what this turning of the Wheel is asking of you specifically.

____

____

WHAT IS ENDING

Name the small closing for this turning point — a project, a season, a way of working you no longer need to carry.

____

____

WHAT IS BEGINNING

A specific opening commitment for the next eighth of the year.

____

____

OSTARA

Ostara is the equinox of Becoming — equal light and dark, the moment when what was hidden begins to break ground. This sabbat asks what is now ready to be visible, and what is still asking for protection.

WHAT THIS SEASON IS ASKING

Name what this turning of the Wheel is asking of you specifically.

____

____

____

WHAT IS ENDING

Name the small closing for this turning point — a project, a season, a way of working you no longer need to carry.

____

____

____

WHAT IS BEGINNING

A specific opening commitment for the next eighth of the year.

____

____

BELTANE

Beltane is the first fullness — Becoming has ripened into Authority. This sabbat asks where you are now governing, and whether your governance is alive or merely held.

WHAT THIS SEASON IS ASKING

Name what this turning of the Wheel is asking of you specifically.

____

____

WHAT IS ENDING

Name the small closing for this turning point — a project, a season, a way of working you no longer need to carry.

____

____

WHAT IS BEGINNING

A specific opening commitment for the next eighth of the year.

____

____

LITHA

Litha is the longest light — Authority at its fullest. This sabbat asks whether your authority is sustainable, or whether it is borrowing from a Return that has not yet been honored.

WHAT THIS SEASON IS ASKING

Name what this turning of the Wheel is asking of you specifically.

WHAT IS ENDING

Name the small closing for this turning point — a project, a season, a way of working you no longer need to carry.

WHAT IS BEGINNING

A specific opening commitment for the next eighth of the year.

LAMMAS

Lammas is the first harvest — Offering begins. This sabbat asks what is now ripe enough to be given, and what is being given before its time.

WHAT THIS SEASON IS ASKING

Name what this turning of the Wheel is asking of you specifically.

____

____

____

WHAT IS ENDING

Name the small closing for this turning point — a project, a season, a way of working you no longer need to carry.

____

____

____

WHAT IS BEGINNING

A specific opening commitment for the next eighth of the year.

____

____

____

MABON

Mabon is the equinox of Offering — what has been given returns as gratitude or as cost. This sabbat asks what your offerings have actually produced, and what the offering has cost.

WHAT THIS SEASON IS ASKING

Name what this turning of the Wheel is asking of you specifically.

WHAT IS ENDING

Name the small closing for this turning point — a project, a season, a way of working you no longer need to carry.

WHAT IS BEGINNING

A specific opening commitment for the next eighth of the year.

SAMHAIN

Samhain is the threshold of Return — the door into the dark half of the year. This sabbat asks what is ending, and whether you have the structure to let it end.

WHAT THIS SEASON IS ASKING

Name what this turning of the Wheel is asking of you specifically.

____

____

____

WHAT IS ENDING

Name the small closing for this turning point — a project, a season, a way of working you no longer need to carry.

____

____

____

WHAT IS BEGINNING

A specific opening commitment for the next eighth of the year.

____

____

YULE

Yule is the deepest Return — longest night, lowest light, fallow consolidation. This sabbat asks what the dark has taught, and what is quietly preparing to begin again.

WHAT THIS SEASON IS ASKING

Name what this turning of the Wheel is asking of you specifically.

____

____

____

WHAT IS ENDING

Name the small closing for this turning point — a project, a season, a way of working you no longer need to carry.

____

____

____

WHAT IS BEGINNING

A specific opening commitment for the next eighth of the year.

____

____

WHAT HAS ACTUALLY HAPPENED

*A quarter of the year has passed. This page is for the backward look —
what happened, what shifted, what the season taught — and a short
forward look at what the next quarter is now asking.*

Becoming · Imbolc through Ostara

WHAT THIS QUARTER HAS HELD

*The shape of the season as it actually unfolded — offerings made, offerings refused,
withdrawals kept, withdrawals lost.*

____

____

____

WHAT THE SEASON HAS TAUGHT

What you know now about your timing that you did not know three months ago.

____

____

____

WHAT HAS ACTUALLY HAPPENED

*A quarter of the year has passed. This page is for the backward look —
what happened, what shifted, what the season taught — and a short
forward look at what the next quarter is now asking.*

Authority · Beltane through Litha

WHAT THIS QUARTER HAS HELD

*The shape of the season as it actually unfolded — offerings made, offerings refused,
withdrawals kept, withdrawals lost.*

____

____

____

____

WHAT THE SEASON HAS TAUGHT

What you know now about your timing that you did not know three months ago.

____

____

____

____

WHAT HAS ACTUALLY HAPPENED

*A quarter of the year has passed. This page is for the backward look —
what happened, what shifted, what the season taught — and a short
forward look at what the next quarter is now asking.*

Offering · Lammas through Mabon

WHAT THIS QUARTER HAS HELD

*The shape of the season as it actually unfolded — offerings made, offerings refused,
withdrawals kept, withdrawals lost.*

____

____

____

____

WHAT THE SEASON HAS TAUGHT

What you know now about your timing that you did not know three months ago.

____

____

____

____

WHAT HAS ACTUALLY HAPPENED

*A quarter of the year has passed. This page is for the backward look —
what happened, what shifted, what the season taught — and a short
forward look at what the next quarter is now asking.*

Return · Samhain through Yule

WHAT THIS QUARTER HAS HELD

*The shape of the season as it actually unfolded — offerings made, offerings refused,
withdrawals kept, withdrawals lost.*

____

____

____

WHAT THE SEASON HAS TAUGHT

What you know now about your timing that you did not know three months ago.

____

____

____

YEAR-END

INTEGRATION

You named the wound in Part Two. You built tools in Part Three. You used them for a year. This page is where the year speaks back.

THE WOUND, THEN

The sentence you wrote at the end of Part Two — write it here again, in the same words.

____

____

____

THE WOUND, NOW

A year of using the tools. Where is the wound now? What has shifted, what is the same, what has become something else?

____

____

____

____

WHAT THE YEAR TAUGHT ABOUT TIMING

Not what you intended to learn. What the year actually showed you — including what you would rather not have learned.

____

____

____

____

____

____

____

THE QUESTION THE NEXT YEAR CARRIES

One sentence. The question the next year of timing is asking you to live.

____

____

____

CLOSING

AFTER THE WORKBOOK

The workbook ends here. The timing wound does not — it shifts shape, relaxes its grip in some places, tightens in others, and the work of recognizing where in the Wheel you are continues as long as the Wheel keeps turning.

You can return to any part of this workbook at any time. The Season Finder is a tool for whenever your timing feels misaligned. The Wheel Plan can be redrawn each year. The repair tools you built in Part Three are yours to revise. The journal you have just filled becomes the record you read back when you have lost your bearings.

You do not need this book to live this work. You needed it once, to name what you could not yet name. Now you have named it. The naming is yours.

The Wheel turns.
You are not asked to make it turn.
You are asked to live where in its turning you are.

— end of the workbook —

GLOSSARY OF TERMS

The vocabulary this workbook uses, grouped by the concepts it describes. Where a term appears repeatedly across the parts, this is where to come back to remind yourself what it points to.

THE FOUR SEASONS OF THE GOD'S ARC

● BECOMING

The first phase. Something is forming but is not yet ready to be seen or given. Becoming asks for protection, slowness, and the patience to let what is forming take its own shape. Its violation is being demanded to perform before it has formed.

● AUTHORITY

The phase of governing what has begun. Authority is steady, sustaining, holding continuity. Its discipline is governance; its distortion is overfunctioning — holding past the point where holding is needed.

● OFFERING

The phase of delivering what has ripened. A true Offering has a gate: it opens deliberately, closes deliberately, and is marked publicly. Its violation is continuous giving — the offering that has no end becomes depletion.

● RETURN

The phase of withdrawal, fallow, restoration. Return is what makes the next Becoming possible. Its discipline is consolidation; its violation is avoidance, or — more often — a refusal to let Return actually be Return.

THE WOUND AND ITS ANATOMY

THE TIMING WOUND

The structural condition that forms when a life is asked to offer continuously, without the sacred withdrawal an arc requires to complete. Not a personal failing — a structural problem of how most contemporary lives are organized.

SACRED TIME

Time that does not produce. Time set apart for Return, fallow, threshold, ritual. The opposite of productivity time. When sacred time collapses, an arc cannot complete; it only repeats.

PREMATURE SACRIFICE

Offering from a seed that has not yet ripened. The most common timing wound. Work delivered before it is ready, relationships committed to before their foundations have set, bodies taxed before their strength is built.

THE FOUR REPAIR TOOLS

THE RHYTHM RULE

A structural rule about the shape of time — when work is active, when withdrawal is sacred, where the gates between them sit. Pre-decided, non-negotiable. It works because it does not require willpower in the moment.

THE GATE

The structural mark of a completed Offering. A real gate opens deliberately, closes deliberately, and marks the closing publicly. Without a gate, an offering bleeds into the next without ever ending.

THE CONSTRAINT CLAUSE

A sentence written before pressure arrives, declaring in advance what you will and will not do when demand increases. The clause takes the decision out of the moment, because the deciding has already happened.

THE CLOSING RITE & VOW

The central repair structure. The Closing Rite names and releases what is ending — an offering, a season, a role. The Vow names what is committed to in what begins. Together they mark a real threshold: not "I am tired now" but "this arc is complete, and another is beginning."

STRUCTURAL VOCABULARY

THE SEASON FINDER

The three-step diagnostic used repeatedly across the year. Step One names your global season. Step Two maps how that season is showing up across each domain of your life. Step Three reads the pattern.

THE PERSONAL WHEEL PLAN

A structural map of the year — which domains are in which season, where Offerings will likely occur, and where Return must be scheduled. Drafted once at the year's beginning and revised quarterly.

THE GOD'S ARC

The theological backbone of the framework. The four phases — Becoming, Authority, Offering, Return — as they appear in the annual procession of the Wheel of the Year, and as they recur in every smaller arc within a life. Developed more fully in *The Timing Wound* proper.

THE WHEEL OF THE YEAR

The cyclical structure of eight sabbats — Imbolc, Ostara, Beltane, Litha, Lammas, Mabon, Samhain, Yule — that anchor the four seasons of the God's arc to specific points in the solar year. The Wheel turns whether or not we recognize it.

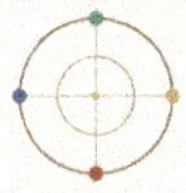

THE CLOSING RITE

What I now close

____

____

____

What I release with it

____

____

____

THE VOW

What I now begin

____

____

____

What I vow

THE CLOSING RITE

What I now close

____

____

____

What I release with it

____

____

____

THE VOW

What I now begin

____

____

____

What I vow

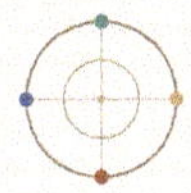

THE CLOSING RITE

What I now close

____

____

____

What I release with it

____

____

____

THE VOW

What I now begin

____

____

____

What I vow

CONTINUING THE WORK

The timing wound is one entry point into the larger work that Grist publishes — a polytheist theology of how to live inside cyclical time. If the framework you have just worked with felt useful, three other Grist titles offer related instruments for adjacent questions.

HOURS

A Theology of Sacred Time

Where this workbook addresses the annual arc, *Hours* works at a different scale — the daily and the eternal. It maps the architecture of sacred time itself: the four directions of the day, the four orientations of the barque, the rites that hold each register. Free as a Grist lead title, with companion printable workbook and audio.

BELTANE

A Theology of First Fullness

The first sabbat-specific volume in Grist's *Turn* library. Beltane names the moment Becoming ripens into Authority — what it is to govern from your own fullness, what makes that fullness different from depletion. Includes paperback, ebook, audiobook, and printable companion planner with subliminal alchemy audio.

PENTACLES

A Theology of Matter and the Authority of What Endures

The first volume of Grist's *Arcana Library*, treating the suit of Pentacles as a theology of embodiment, material reality, and the slow authority of what lasts. Especially relevant to readers whose timing wound concerns the body, the home, or the work of making something that does not pass. Available in paperback, ebook, audio, and as a meditation series.

COLOPHON

———

The Timing Wound: A Workbook
was designed and set in three typefaces:
Cinzel for display headings,
EB Garamond for body text,
and *Raleway* for editorial captions.

The wheel glyph and the corner brackets
are part of the visual vocabulary of Grist,
a polytheist publishing imprint
founded by Kristi Hall.

———

The work, as ever, is the Wheel's.
The naming is ours.

———